17 ROADBLOCKS ON THE HIGHWAY OF LIFE
AND HOW TO MOVE AROUND THEM

By Brian L. Harbour

Smyth & Helwys Publishing, Inc.
6316 Peake Road
Macon, Georgia 31210-3960
1-800-747-3016
©2005 by Smyth & Helwys Publishing
All rights reserved.
Printed in the United States of America.

The paper used in this publication meets the minimum requirements of
American National Standard for Information Sciences—
Permanence of Paper for Printed Library Materials.
ANSI Z39.48–1984. (alk. paper)

Library of Congress Cataloging-in-Publication Data

Harbour, Brian L.
17 roadblocks on the highway of life : and how to move around them
by Brian L. Harbour.
p. cm.
ISBN 1-57312-447-8 (pbk. : alk. paper)
1. Christian life.
I. Title.
II. Title: Seventeen roadblocks on the highway of life.
BV4501.3.H365 2005
248.4—dc22

2005005899

Contents

Foreword

Dr. Brian Harbour's book, *17 Roadblocks on the Highway of Life and How to Move Around Them*, is on target in addressing some of the obstacles each of us face in life. These obstacles are real, but they do not have the capacity to be permanent roadblocks in our journey on the highway of life.

Brian's book offers sensitivity to the things each of us has to face. While no person would probably face all of the roadblocks, each of us will face some of them.

The great thing about this book is that Brian not only lists the roadblocks. He also goes to Scripture to share what the Bible says about each specific situation. He then walks through the meaning of these Scriptures for the particular roadblocks.

Brian Harbour goes a step further to list specific strategies we can use to move around these roadblocks. I have read many books in which people are able to list the problem and tell how the Bible addresses the problem, but seldom do we have access to the mind of a writer who really gives an application of the Scripture and specific strategies of how to deal with certain situations.

This book will not only be a tremendous asset to me and to readers, but it is also something I can share with people I encounter who are facing some of these roadblocks. It is written in a style that is simple enough for everybody to understand, but the concepts are so deeply profound that they deal with the source of our problem. The writing style of Brian Harbour is winsome, understandable, encouraging, and convicting.

This book can also be used as a discipleship tool as it speaks directly to people who are on the journey of faith. Finally, it is a great evangelistic tool as it can be shared with unchurched people who are facing these roadblocks.

John Ed Mathison
Senior Minister
Frazer United Methodist Church
Montgomery, Alabama

Introduction

One afternoon about a year ago, my wife Jan and I went early to the opening of a much-publicized movie in order to beat the crowd. The parking lot was packed, however, so I dropped Jan off and looked for a place to park. Driving down one lane, I noticed a car pulling out of a space. Another car approached from the opposite direction, but I was there first, so when the car pulled out, I rushed into the parking place and headed into the movie. After the movie, I found a *Driver's Handbook* resting on the front windshield of my car with this note scribbled on it: "You took my parking place. That was rude. Read this book. Maybe it will help you do better next time!"

That experience was at the back of my mind as I formulated the plan for this book. Even though Jesus promised to give us abundant life when we connect our lives with his, most of us as Christians do not experience the fullness of that life. Why? Because we allow various roadblocks to sidetrack us in our journey. Consequently, we often need a handbook to show us how to navigate our lives more effectively.

This book presents several learning tracks. To begin with, I identify a series of scriptures that addresses each of the roadblocks; then, I draw from those scriptures lessons to guide our way. Next, I offer a cameo of someone in the Bible who illustrates these scripture lessons. These biblical models show us how to navigate successfully through life. Also, in each chapter, I offer specific strategies for implementing these scriptural lessons. This multiple-track approach should provide a rich resource as we face these roadblocks in our own lives.

I would suggest two approaches to the book. First, read through the entire book to get an overview of the material. Then, keep the book in reach of your desk so you can refer to individual chapters as you encounter specific roadblocks. A Quick Review at the back of the book provides an easy reference to identify the Scriptures and strategies that relate to each roadblock.

Special thanks go to my administrative assistant Beth Grafton; to my son, Collin Harbour; and to my friend Lora Burnett. Each contributed to the book—Beth with her typing of manuscripts, Collin with his eye for detail and form, and Lora with her grammatical and practical suggestions. The book is better because of them.

Brian Harbour
Richardson, Texas

When We Want Too Much Too Soon

The Ambition Roadblock

Chuck and Mary Gordy are among the best friends my wife Jan and I have ever had. They were members of the church in Jackson, Mississippi, where I was a pastor more than thirty years ago. They have four children (three boys and a girl), just as we do. They were our vacation partners for years. We've helped raise each other's kids. I've performed the weddings for their children. Consequently, the relationships go deep and the memories are pleasurable.

One of my favorite memories is of a pizza place in Jackson. Brent Gordy was about ten at the time. He and a friend were eating pizza when Jan and I went in to grab a bite. As I walked by Brent's table, I reached down and picked up a piece of his pizza, took a big bite out of it, and then dropped it back on his plate. I slapped him on the back and said, "Thanks, Brent," and we went on to our table. A little while later, as Brent and his friend left, he brought a piece of pizza to me and said, "Here's another one if you want it. I was too full to eat it all." (A ten-year-old boy who couldn't eat all of his pizza should have raised my suspicion!) Our pizza had still not come, so I thanked him and took the piece of pizza. I bit in and was ready to swallow when I realized I had made a huge mistake. As I spit the bite of pizza into a napkin, I caught Brent in my peripheral vision bent over laughing. Quickly, I figured out what had happened. Brent had doused the piece of pizza with Tabasco sauce. A touch of Tabasco sauce is great. It really adds flavor to food. However, it doesn't take much Tabasco sauce to be too much.

Ambition is like that. A little ambition is good, for ambition gives flavor to a person's life. On the other hand, nothing is blander than a person with no ambition. Consider, for example, this tale of two generations. Father and teenage son were talking.

Father: Son, why don't you get a job?
Son: Why?
Father: So you can earn some money.
Son: Why?
Father: So you can put some money in a bank account and earn interest.
Son: Why?
Father: So that when you're old you can use the money you have saved to
      live on and you won't ever have to work again.
Son: I'm not working now!

A lack of ambition in a person is distressing. That's why I stated above that ambition is good. I would go further to claim that ambition is in fact an essential part of life. However, when ambition evolves into drivenness, it moves beyond something we control and instead controls us. Drivenness, according to Drs. Robert Hemfelt, Frank Minirth, and Paul Meier, "is an insatiable drive to do more and be more." They explain, "It's a drive that may be masked by charitable and positive motives, but in reality originates in deep, perhaps even unconscious, feelings of inadequacy and shame." They conclude that drivenness "may be the most prominent emotional illness of the 1990s."[1]

The right kind of ambition is a positive motivator in life. Ambition can become a roadblock, however, when we want too much too soon and ambition morphs into drivenness. The key is to find the balance between enough ambition and too much ambition so we can navigate around the roadblock of drivenness.

Search the Scripture

For the Christian, the place to begin seeking answers to this dilemma is within God's word. In the Scripture, we find several helpful insights into the danger of too much ambition.

- Psalm 119:36-37: "Turn my heart toward your statutes and not toward selfish gain. Turn my eyes away from worthless things; preserve my life according to your word."
- Luke 12:15: "Watch out! Be on your guard against all kinds of greed; a man's life does not consist in the abundance of his possessions."
- Romans 12:3: "For by the grace given me I say to every one of you: Do not think of yourself more highly than you ought, but rather think of yourself with sober judgment, in accordance with the measure of faith God has given you."
- Philippians 4:11: "I am not saying this because I am in need, for I have learned to be content whatever the circumstances."
- 1 Timothy 6:10: "For the love of money is a root of all kinds of evil. Some people, eager for money, have wandered from the faith and pierced themselves with many griefs."
- Hebrews 13:5-6: "Through Jesus, therefore, let us continually offer to God a sacrifice of praise—the fruit of lips that confess his name. And do not forget to do good and to share with others, for with such sacrifices God is pleased."

These Scriptures remind us of some of the reasons for our drivenness. The psalmist suggests that one of the reasons for uncontrolled ambition is a focus on the wrong things. Focusing on what we can get for ourselves instead of focusing on what we can do for God creates uncontrolled ambition (Ps 119:36-37). Paul revealed another source of uncontrolled ambition in Romans 12:3: an exalted opinion of ourselves. Failure to recognize the limitations of our lives will drive us to attempt activities we are not equipped to accomplish.

These Scriptures also acknowledge the irony of our drivenness. For example, Jesus reminded us that fulfilling our ambition and obtaining all the things we want will not necessarily bring satisfaction (Luke 12:15). We can get what we want and then discover that we don't want what we've got. Or, to put it another way, a person can get to the top of the ladder of success and discover that the ladder is leaning against the wrong wall.

In addition, these Scriptures reflect on the nature of our drivenness. Drivenness is fed by both an internal source (our attitude) and an external source (materialism). Overcoming our drivenness requires that we address both aspects of the problem. Paul kept his ambition under control by replacing an attitude of greed with an attitude of gratitude (Phil 4:11). In the same way, thankfulness for what we are and have will deflate ambition run amok. But we must also address the external source, materialism. Materialism is one of the marks of our age. Apparently, it was also troublesome in the first century world, even among Christians. In both the 1 Timothy passage (6:10) and the Hebrews passage (13:5-6), the biblical writers warn the first century Christians against an infatuation with money. Likewise for us, love for money must be overshadowed by a higher love—love for God (Matt 6:33).

Scripture instructs us not only with its specific teachings but also by presenting models who flesh out these principles in their lives. Or, in some cases, these models show what happens when a person fails to flesh out these principles. A prime biblical example of someone who was driven by out-of-control ambition was Absalom, the son of David.

Absalom seemed to be the most ambitious of David's children. Absalom's ambition appears in 2 Samuel 15. He provided for himself a chariot and horses and fifty men as runners before him (v. 1). This was the way a king traveled, in a chariot with men running before him. Absalom, therefore, assumed the appearance of a king. He also sat by the gate and gave judgments for those who would normally come to the king for judgment (v. 2). This was the king's responsibility. By acting like the king, Absalom claimed to be king. And Absalom was not innocent in his activities. Instead, he was working out an intentional plan to win the hearts of the people (v. 6). When he felt that he had sufficient support, Absalom rallied his men and moved toward Jerusalem to remove his father from the throne and to take over as king of Israel (vv. 7-12). He not only acted like a king and claimed to be a king. He was determined to become king.

Absalom had many opportunities as the son of the king. However, these were not enough. He wanted to be king, and he wanted to be king now. Ambition drove him to overreach his abilities. Eventually, Absalom lost his life.

In an Andy Capp cartoon strip, Andy tells his beleaguered wife Flo, "I'm not worth anything. I'm not good for anything." Flo responds, "Don't be so hard on yourself. If nothing else, you serve as a horrible example." In much the same way, Absalom serves as a horrible example of the kind of drivenness to avoid.

Set the Strategy

These Scriptures and the negative model of Absalom focus on the roadblock of uncontrolled ambition and provide resources from which we can develop specific strategies.

Strategy #1 is to *determine the source of our "drivenness."* Drivenness in our lives usually arises in one of four ways:

(1) *As a Corrective.* A woman recalled an incident in her childhood that became a defining moment in her life. She grew up in a poor family and consequently they never had much. One year at school, around Christmas time, the teacher called her and a few of her classmates out of the classroom and took them to the cafeteria, where a lady in sparkling clothes presented a gift to her and the other "underprivileged" children. As she received the gift from the benevolent lady, she said to herself, "Someday, I'm going to be the one giving Christmas gifts to the poor." She was driven all her life by the desire to correct the poverty in which she was reared. Her motto was "I want more than this. I'm going to be different. Just watch me."

(2) *As Compensation.* I have a friend who has worked his whole life to make up for the approval his father never gave him. Whatever he did was never enough. His father never expressed approval for what he did. A few years ago, his father committed suicide, adding to the unsolved problem of a young man who never felt he was quite good enough. The drivenness of my friend's life is an attempt to compensate for the approval he never received. His motto is "I'm worth something whether my father thought so or not. I'm going to be successful; I'll show him."

(3) *From Competition.* A competitive athlete went to the doctor. The doctor said, "You have a temperature of 103." The athlete responded, "What's the record?" Some people are driven by the desire to outdo everyone else. Their motto is "I'm the best. Nobody can do it like I can do it."

(4) *Because of Confusion.* A decade ago our nation was absorbed for months in the trial of O. J. Simpson. The story that unfolded on the television screen unveiled a man who always wanted more—more money, more adulation, and more power—and he would do anything to obtain it. At the heart of the O. J. tragedy was a man so driven that he became confused about right and wrong. Some people are similarly confused about what is right and what is wrong. Their motto is "The end justifies the means. I have a right to these things, no matter what I have to do to get them."

Most drivenness comes from these four sources: completion, compensation, competition, and confused values. The beginning point in moving around our uncontrolled ambition is to determine where it comes from.

Strategy #2 is to *develop the proper response to the cause of our drivenness.* If our drivenness comes from the desire to complete something missing in our lives, then the remedy is to learn how *to accept ourselves as we are.* If our drivenness comes from an attempt to compensate for a lack of approval or affirmation from significant others, then the remedy is to *accept the affirmation of God's love.* If our drivenness comes from a competitiveness to be the best, then the remedy is to *aim for doing our best rather than being the best.* If our drivenness comes from a confusion of values, then the remedy is to *align our goals with God's value system.* Our responses should be tailored to the cause of the drivenness.

Strategy #3 is to *acknowledge and accept the limitations of life.* Ultimately, drivenness is a denial that our lives are limited in any way. But eventually, life will deny our denial—by a breakdown in our health, by the deterioration of our physical bodies, or by the continued changes around us that we are no longer able to keep up with.

In her book *First Ladies,* Margaret Truman presents an intimate portrait of some of the wives of the presidents, revealing the unique privileges and the common problems of the families of those who filled the president's office. Particularly poignant is her account of the death of Calvin and Grace Coolidge's son, Calvin Jr. In an afternoon game of tennis on the White House courts, Calvin Jr. acquired a blister on his big toe. The blister became infected and, because of the limitations of medicine at that time, the family and physicians could only watch helplessly as Calvin Jr. died of blood poisoning. Margaret Truman says Calvin Jr.'s father was particularly tormented by the incongruity of being President of the United States, with all the pomp and power of the office, yet lacking the power to help his dying son. "When he was suffering, he begged me to help him," the President agonized, "but I could not."[2]

In less dramatic ways, life confronts all of us with our limitations. We quickly learn that we can't do everything or solve every problem or attain every goal. We can't be the best at everything. In fact, we can't even be the best at anything for long. Life's limitations affect all of us. Acknowledging and accepting those limitations are keys to moving around the roadblock of drivenness.

Final Word

The challenge facing us as Christians is not to kill our ambition but rather to control it and channel it. If we don't, our misdirected ambition will become a roadblock that prevents us from being what God wants us to be and doing what God wants us to do.

Prayer

Gracious Father
Forgive us
When we confuse
Wants with needs and
What's ours
With what's yours.

Slow us down
So we can enjoy
The abundance
We already have.

Help us to find contentment
Not in what we have in ourselves
But in who we are in you.

And help us to love you
Not for what you can give us
But for who you are.

Amen.

NOTES

[1] Dr. Robert Hemfelt, Dr. Frank Minirth, and Dr. Paul Meier, *We Are Driven: The Compulsive Behaviors America Applauds* (Nashville: Thomas Nelson Publishers, 1991), 6.

[2] Margaret Truman, *First Ladies* (New York: Random House, 1995), 252.

When We Get Good and Mad

The Anger Roadblock

A man was driving down the road when another driver tried to cut in front of him. The offended driver got mad, and then he decided to get even. So he pulled up behind the other car, almost close enough to bump it. The other driver quickly sped up. The offended driver pulled up behind him again, and the other driver sped up again. Finally, they were driving at such a high rate of speed that the man who wanted to get even lost control of his car. It overturned and rolled over four women who were walking along the shoulder of the road. Three of the women were killed!

This is certainly a dramatic story. But it is also an accurate picture of the high cost of anger. Often, as we go through life, people do things or say things that push our hot button, and we get good and mad as a result. Often, relationships and even lives can be destroyed in the aftermath of our anger. James reminded us in his epistle why this kind of anger needs to be controlled (Jas 1:20). The various translations attribute two distinct meanings to this verse.

The Phillips Bible translates the verse this way: "Man's temper is never the means for achieving God's true goodness." In this case, James was suggesting that our anger adversely affects the ongoing of God's kingdom by countering the good news of God. Jesus proclaimed the good news of God's love for all people. Our anger toward others can short-circuit that message, for instead of communicating to the world the loving, accepting, and redeeming kind of love God wants them to feel, we communicate judgment and condemnation. Consequently, our anger hurts God's cause.

The Living Bible translates the phrase like this: "For anger doesn't make us good, as God demands that we must be." In this case, James was not emphasizing what our anger does to God's kingdom but what it does to us. Personal resentment, manifest in anger toward others, robs us of God's forgiving mercy and uplifting power. It chokes off our spiritual life. An old proverb suggests, "Whom the gods would destroy they first make mad." That's another way of saying that our uncontrolled anger will eventually destroy us.

The problem with anger then is twofold. Anger deflects attention from God's kingdom and diminishes our spiritual power. In both instances, it becomes a roadblock that keeps us from experiencing the full and abundant life God wants us to experience through Jesus Christ. Moving around this roadblock on the highway of life means learning how to control our anger.

Search the Scripture

For the Christian, the place to begin seeking answers is within God's word. The Bible repeatedly speaks to the issue of anger. Note the following examples.

- Job 5:2: "For vexation slays the foolish man, and anger kills the simple."
- Proverbs 14:17a: "A quick-tempered man acts foolishly."
- Proverbs 16:32: "He who is slow to anger is better than the mighty, and he who rules his spirit, than he who captures a city."
- Proverbs 19:19: "A man of great anger shall bear the penalty, for if you rescue him, you will only have to do it again."
- Proverbs 25:28: "Like a city that is broken into and without walls is a man who has no control over his spirit."
- Ecclesiastes 7:9: "Do not be eager in your heart to be angry, for anger resides in the bosom of fools."
- Ephesians 4:26: "Do not let the sun go down on your anger."
- James 1:20: "For the anger of man does not achieve the righteousness of God."

These Scriptures remind us that anger can be destructive (Jas 1:20, TLB). According to one newspaper article, anger is implicated especially in heart disease. The writer stated, "Of all the emotional facets that heart patients might show, this one [anger] appears most prominent."[1]

Anger is not only destructive for us. It is also destructive for those who are around us (Job 5:2; Prov 25:28). I heard James Pleitz tell a story about a farmer in Mississippi. As the farmer plowed his corn, he noticed a mouse gnawing away at a stalk. The farmer thought about the long hours he had spent clearing the field and planting and cultivating it. And now this mouse was trying to destroy it. He angrily jumped off his tractor. He picked up a stick and went after the mouse. He beat and slashed and chased and sweated until finally he dealt the mouse a lethal blow. He felt a smug sense of satisfaction until he began to look around and realized that he had destroyed nearly half an acre of corn trying to kill one mouse that couldn't have eaten more than three stalks in an entire season! Anger is, as a country preacher put it, only one letter short of "danger."

In addition, these Scriptures indicate that anger can be addictive. Expressed anger creates a vicious circle that will continually repeat itself unless the circle is broken (Prov 19:19). Gary Collins cites a study of children who were allowed to express their anger. They were encouraged to play with violent toys, to kick the furniture, to freely express their pent-up anger. After doing this, the boys were found to be angrier than they had been at the beginning.[2] Venting our anger does not make it go away. More often, venting simply fuels our anger and makes it worse. Tony Campolo expressed this truth in these words: "Expressing an emotion often causes us to feel the emotion even more intensely. Those who do loving acts usually feel love all the more. Those who do kind things usually end up feeling kind. And those who express anger usually end up feeling more anger. It may be healthier to express anger than to suppress it, but expressing anger usually intensifies it."[3]

Further, these Scriptures affirm that anger can be controlled (Eph 4:26). I am not talking about the anger impulse but the management of our anger impulse. The anger impulse is our physiological response to threat. What we do with that anger impulse is our anger management strategy. In Ephesians 4:26, Paul is talking about the management of this physiological response to our anger, not about the physiological response itself. The response is instinctive; the response to the response is intentional.

Scripture teaches us not just by presenting principles but also by providing models of human beings who faced, and in many instances moved around, these same roadblocks we face today. For example, Joseph was a biblical hero who learned how to manage his anger (Gen 38–45). When Joseph's brothers sold him into slavery, they robbed him of his life of leisure and luxury, with apparently little remorse. Years later, Joseph was in a position to gain his revenge and to vent his anger toward these siblings who had tried to end his life. He avoided the two extremes to which we often go in dealing with our anger.

First, Joseph *did not deny the reason for his anger.* In Genesis 42, after long years of separation, Joseph reconnects with his brothers. However, they do not recognize him now that he is the prime minister of Egypt. Joseph eventually forgave them, but he did not offer forgiveness initially or instantaneously as if nothing had happened. Instead, he wanted to know if they had changed. He wanted to know if their hearts had been softened, or if they were still the hardhearted people who could sell a brother into slavery.

So Joseph planned a test for his brothers. He demanded that they bring their youngest brother Benjamin back to Egypt. To enforce his demand, he imprisoned Simeon until they came back with Benjamin. Fast-forward to a later time when, after a long delay, the brothers returned to Egypt with their brother Benjamin, just as the prime Mmnister of Egypt had demanded. On their return, Joseph gave them the grain they needed and sent them back home. The brothers thought they had averted the crisis that seemed to be only a slight misstep away.

However, Joseph planted his golden cup in Benjamin's sack. His men then overtook his brothers, found the cup in Benjamin's sack, and brought the brothers back to Egypt. Joseph announced that he would keep Benjamin as his slave but that the rest of them could go free. At that point, Judah pled for Benjamin's freedom and even offered himself in place of Benjamin. Joseph thus concluded that his brothers had changed. Having dealt with the deep emotional scars on his own life and having sorted through the emotional condition of his brothers, Joseph was now ready to move forward with his plan for reconciliation.

Secondly, Joseph *did not allow his anger to lead him into destructive actions.* He could have had all his brothers killed in return for what they had done to him. He had both the power and the authority to do it. However, he was unwilling to release his anger in a destructive way. Instead, he forgave his brothers and was finally restored to his family.

Either of the extreme reactions to anger is deadly. Repressing our anger and thus refusing to deal with its cause allows our anger to fester into the poison of depression. On the other hand, venting our anger in a destructive way allows our anger to explode into a force of destruction. Joseph demonstrated how to avoid those destructive responses and instead control anger.

Set the Strategy

Using these lessons from Scripture and the insights from Joseph's response to his brothers, let me offer strategies for moving around the roadblock of uncontrolled anger in our lives.

Strategy #1 is to *delay the expression of our anger.* In his epistle, James suggests two simple steps in this delay strategy. On the one hand, we are to "be swift to hear" (Jas 1:19). One translation renders the phrase: "Be a ready listener" (Amplified). When anger arises about someone or something, our initial response should be to listen. Listening carefully and completely will enable us to understand better what was said, to understand more clearly what the person actually did and why, and to discern more accurately the context out of which the person spoke. Thus, listening carefully delays the expression of our anger.

On the other hand, James challenged us to "be slow to speak" (Jas 1:19). Our immediate reaction to a situation and our reaction after thinking through the situation are usually quite different. Allowing our feelings to settle enables us to take a more rational look at the situation before responding. And taking a more rational look saves us from immediate reactions that are not carefully thought through.

An incident during the Civil War illustrates this truth. On one occasion, Secretary of War Harold M. Stanton complained to Abraham Lincoln of a major general in the Union Army who had accused Stanton of favoritism in extremely abusive language. Lincoln suggested writing him a sharp rejoinder. "Hit him hard!" he said. Stanton at once wrote out a strongly worded letter and showed it to the president. "Right! Right!" cried Lincoln approvingly. "Just it! Score him deeply! That's first rate, Stanton!" But when Stanton folded the letter and put it in an envelope, Lincoln interrupted him. "What are you going to do with it?" he asked. "Send it," Stanton replied in surprise. "Nonsense!" exclaimed Lincoln. "You don't want to send that letter. Put it in the stove. That's what I do when I have written a letter while I am angry. It's a good letter and you've had a good time writing it, and you feel better. Now, burn it, and write another letter."[4]

Use a similar approach that will save you from your immediate response. When anger arises, delay the expression of it.

Strategy #2 is to *define the reason for our anger.* Conventional wisdom suggests counting to ten before expressing our anger. Delay is an excellent strategy. However, the point is not simply to count during this delay but instead to define why and at whom we are angry. Defining the reasons for our anger enables us to give a response that is more congruent with the problem. Identifying the target of our anger enables us to respond to the right person instead of spewing out on others the wrath we really feel toward ourselves.

I remember a cartoon that showed two men talking. One said, "Well, they shot my dog Fido today." The other responded, "Oh, was he mad?" To which the first man responded, "Well, he wasn't too pleased about it!" Which reminds me of a witticism I once read: "Killing the dog does not cure the bite!"

Taking time to discern the reason for our anger will enable us to avoid responding in the wrong way to the wrong person. Then our response can be directed at the true source of our anger and can address the true reason for our anger.

Strategy #3 is to *destroy the root of our anger.* Perhaps the most important strategy in dealing with our anger response is to try to nip our anger in the bud before it actually triggers a regrettable event.

One way to destroy the root of our anger is to change our circumstances. Sometimes, as the old saying goes, "people lose their temper because they get needled by the spur of the moment." In other words, their anger arises from their circumstances. If that is the case with us, the solution is to change our circumstances if we can. For example, the proper response to a relationship that continuously generates anger is to break off the relationship. The proper response to an activity that arouses us to anger is to cease participating in that activity. We have choices in life. And sometimes the best choice is simply to move away from the source of our anger.

On the other hand, if the circumstances can't be changed, the solution is to change our attitude toward the circumstance. If we change our expectations of others, our perceptions of others, and our desires of others, we can change the way we react to things and people outside of us, even when the circumstances themselves cannot be altered.

In cases when the circumstance cannot be altered and when our attitude toward the person connected with that circumstance is so mired in the emotional baggage attached to the circumstance, the solution is simply to release the circumstance and person to God, recognizing that judgment is God's responsibility, not ours.

Final Word

Delaying our anger, defining the reason for our anger, and destroying the source of our anger—these three strategies will help us navigate around the anger roadblock on the highway of life. And this is important because "man's temper is never the means for achieving God's true goodness" (Jas 1:20).

Prayer

God, I cannot separate
My hatred for what was done
From the person who did it.

I despise the deed.
I loathe the person who did the deed.
My rage is my only revenge.

But, God, my rage destroys me too.
I feel this seething anger
Searing my own soul.

O Lord, my God,
Deliver me
From the evil
I would do to myself.

Amen.[5]

NOTES

[1] *Dallas Morning News* (7 June 1993), 3C.

[2] Gary R. Collins, *The Magnificent Mind* (Waco: Word Books, 1985), 77.

[3] Anthony Campolo, *Seven Deadly Sins* (Wheaton IL: Victor Books, 1987), 64.

[4] Paul F. Boller Jr., *Presidential Anecdotes* (New York: Penguin Books, 1981), 135.

[5] Richard Foster, *Prayers from the Heart* (New York: HarperCollins Publishing, 1994).

R O A D B L O C K   # 3

When We're Tied up in Knots

The Anxiety Roadblock

Anxiety has been called "the official emotion of our age."[1] It is universal in its presence. Old and young alike experience it. Men and women find it equally troublesome. It is not an American exclusive but one that finds expression in people of all races and nations. It really is "the official emotion of our age."

Dr. John R. Knapp of Eastern Michigan University ranked these as the top ten causes of anxiety:

(1) Unexpectedly finding your door open upon arriving home at night.
(2) Being an hour late for an important appointment.
(3) Realizing you've forgotten your wallet when it comes time to pay the bill.
(4) Having to speak in front of a crowd.
(5) Interviewing for a job you would really like to have.
(6) Seeing flashing red lights behind you on the highway.
(7) Not being sure that you've locked the back door after having left for an extended time away from home.
(8) Asking for a raise.

(9) Telling your spouse about an automobile accident you've had.
(10) Beginning a new job.[2]

Of course, this is one list of many that identify the causes of anxiety. Whatever your list looks like, all of us have a list of things that create anxiety in our lives. Anxiety is a roadblock that often prevents us from experiencing the abundant life Jesus wants for us. To determine how to navigate around this roadblock on the highway of life, we need to turn first to the Scripture.

Search the Scripture

The Scripture is always the place for the Christian to begin seeking answers for life's roadblocks. Several verses provide insight on how to navigate around the roadblock of anxiety.

- Matthew 6:25: "Do not be anxious for your life, as to what you shall eat, or what you shall drink; nor for your body, as to what you shall put on."
- Matthew 6:34: "Therefore do not be anxious for tomorrow; for tomorrow will care for itself."
- Matthew 13:22: "The worry of the world, and the deceitfulness of riches choke the word, and it becomes unfruitful."
- John 14:1: "Let not your heart be troubled; believe in God, believe also in Me."
- Philippians 4:6-7: "Be anxious for nothing, but in everything by prayer and supplication with thanksgiving let your requests be made known to God, and the peace of God, which surpasses all comprehension, shall guard your hearts and your minds in Christ Jesus."
- 1 Peter 5:6-7: "Humble yourselves, therefore, under the mighty hand of God; that He may exalt you at the proper time, casting all your anxiety upon Him, because He cares for you."

These Scriptures identify some of the sources of anxiety. Sometimes anxiety grows out of our confusion about the value system of the world. That was Jesus' reminder in the Sermon on the Mount. We worry about the material possessions of this world because we have bought into the world's value system (Matt 6:25). At other times, we worry because of uncertainty about the future. Jesus also addressed that issue in the Sermon on the Mount. He reminded us that each day has enough to keep our minds occupied. We shouldn't borrow trouble from tomorrow (Matt 6:34). These are just two of the many sources of anxiety.

Further, these Scriptures remind us of the danger of anxiety. In the parable of the sower and the seeds in Matthew 13, Jesus describes four different kinds of soil upon which the word of God falls. Some seed fell on the path that was so hard the seed never took root but instead was snatched away by the birds. Some seed fell on the rock covered by a thin veneer of soil. These seeds sprouted temporarily but then quickly withered because they had no root. In describing the seeds that fell on the third kind of soil, Jesus connected with the subject of this chapter. These seeds took root and began to grow. However, the plant could not flourish because it was choked out by the worries of the world (Matt 13:22). In the same way, anxiety becomes a negative force in our lives that distracts, distorts, and eventually destroys our lives.

In addition, these Scriptures reveal some of the solutions for anxiety. In John 14:1, for example, Jesus pronounces the primary antidote to the kind of anxiety that pulls our lives apart: trust in a God who loves us and who provides for us, both in this life and in the life to come. In Philippians 4:6-7, Paul identifies prayer as an answer for anxiety. "Do not be anxious about anything," Paul urges the Philippians, "but in everything, by prayer and petition, with thanksgiving, present your requests to God." When we do that, Paul promises, "the peace of God, which transcends all understanding, will guard your hearts and your minds in Christ Jesus." Prayer puts us in touch with a God for whom no problem is unsolvable.

These Scriptures give us a starting point for navigating around the roadblock of anxiety. Further lessons from Scripture come in the biblical models of those who dealt with the same roadblocks we face today. Mary of Bethany provides one of the most intriguing New Testament examples of a person who refused to let anxiety detract her from the joys of the present (Luke 10:38-42). As a result, Jesus especially commended her.

As Jesus traveled around the countryside, he came to a certain village in which two sisters lived: Mary and Martha. Jesus went to eat with them. Mary and Martha responded to his visit in contrasting ways. Mary was so thrilled Jesus was there that she wanted to spend every moment with him. The Bible says, "She sat at the Lord's feet listening to what he said" (Luke 10:39). Martha, on the other hand, was so thrilled Jesus was there that she wanted everything to be just right to host this important visitor. The Bible says she "was distracted by all the preparations that had to be made" (Luke 10:40).

Here is the picture. Mary is sitting at Jesus' feet, listening to him. Martha is in the kitchen making the biscuits, and Martha loses it. She storms into the room where Jesus and Mary are talking, and with obvious irritation says to Jesus, "Lord, don't you care that my sister has left me to do the work by myself? Tell her to help me!" (Luke 10:40). Jesus answers, "Martha, Martha, you are worried and upset about many things, but only one thing is needed. Mary has chosen what is better, and it will not be taken away from her" (Luke 10:41-42).

Actually, some things about that story bother us. Most of us would probably side more with Martha than with Mary. After all, dinner had to be cooked, and the table had to be set, and the dishes had to be washed. Somebody had to do these things. We would most likely praise Martha for doing these necessary things. Jesus, instead, praised Mary because she recognized what was important and what was permanent. Martha was "distracted" because she made what was secondary primary and she was more concerned with the temporary than with the permanent. "Mary has chosen what is better," Jesus said. That's why she is a model for moving past this roadblock called anxiety.

Set the Strategy

From these specific Scriptures and from the example of Mary, we can learn lessons about dealing with anxiety. We must then translate these lessons into specific strategies for our lives today. Here are some strategies to consider.

Strategy #1 is to *refocus.* Many times anxiety develops in a life that is too self-focused. Consequently, one solution for anxiety is to refocus our attention on God. Paul made this point in Philippians 4. Instead of being anxious, Paul called on us to let our requests be known to God "with thanksgiving" (Phil 4:6). When we try to face our problems in our own strength, our inadequacy produces despair. On the other hand, when we bring God into our situation through prayer, we recognize his adequacy. That produces thanksgiving.

Ruth Graham, the wife of Billy Graham, describes a time in her life when she was awakened by her worry about a particular person. Deciding to study the promises of God's word instead of brooding over her problem, she turned to this Philippians 4 passage. She spent time worshiping God. As a result, she said, "It was as if someone suddenly turned on the lights in my mind and heart, and the little fears and worries which, like mice and cockroaches, had been nibbling away in the darkness, suddenly scuttled for cover." She gave this conclusion: "That was when I learned that worship and worry cannot live in the same heart; they are mutually exclusive."[3]

When worry comes, we need to give attention to the promises instead of the problems. We need to refocus.

Strategy #2 is to *clarify*. After getting the proper perspective on God and his promises, the next step is to get the proper perspective on our anxiety. One way to do that is to find humor in our situation. Humor has a way of diffusing even the most monumental problem. President Lincoln demonstrated that on one occasion during the Civil War. With the pressure of the war bearing heavily on his shoulders, the President called in his cabinet. When they sat down, President Lincoln read a spoof on preachers written by Artemus Ward, a humorist of that generation. When the President finished reading the piece, he set down the book and was convulsed in laughter. None of the cabinet members even smiled. Secretary of War Harold Stanton even considered walking out. How could the President be frivolous in such serious times? President Lincoln told his cabinet, "Gentlemen, why don't you laugh? With the fearful strain that is upon me night and day, if I did not laugh I should die. And you need this medicine as much as I."[4] Humor can dilute the force of anxiety. It can untense the intense.

Keeping a worry journal is also a helpful strategy when anxiety has us in its grip. Our entries in our worry journal should include everything that raises anxiety in our lives. Periodically, we should check the list. Typically, we discover that many of the things that wracked us with anxiety never happened. Further, for those things that did happen, our anxiety did not help us deal with them more effectively. In either case, our anxiety was worthless.

One man set aside a worry time each week. He decided he would worry every Wednesday afternoon from 1:00 to 3:00. At any other time, when worry raised its head, he would say to himself, "I'll worry about that on Wednesday afternoon." In most cases, he discovered that by the time Wednesday rolled around, the cause for the worry was gone.

Don't tremble in the presence of your anxiety. Face it head on. Understanding more clearly the nature of our anxiety will enable us to move around it more effectively.

Strategy #3 is to *simplify*. A more proactive step in navigating around our anxiety is to simplify our lives. This step digs deeper into the core of the problem. In most cases, anxiety is directly connected to our ambitions. Consequently, simplifying our lives by changing our value system will lessen our anxiety.

A physician who specialized in stress disorders addressed a group of sales and market executives in Buffalo, New York. He spent forty-four minutes of his forty-five-minute presentation telling entertaining stories. He used his last minute to present his "one-sentence, surefire, cure-all technique that never fails to cure stress-related syndromes." That sounds like a good thing to know. What was his one sentence, cure-all technique for anxiety? "If you want to have less stress in your life," he said, "lower your expectations."[5]

This was Jesus' point in his discussion in Matthew 6. He said to his disciples, "So do not worry, saying, 'What shall we eat?' or 'What shall we drink?' or 'What shall we wear?' For the pagans run after all these things, and your heavenly Father knows that you need them. But seek first his kingdom and his righteousness, and all these things will be given to you as well" (Matt 6:31-32).

Much of our anxiety comes because we have been captivated by the lifestyle of the world. Our ambitions are shaped by desire for the things of the world. In such cases, failure to obtain these things or fear that we might not obtain them becomes the seedbed of anxiety. The answer is to simplify our lives and internalize the lifestyle of the kingdom of God.

Strategy #4 is to *act*. Sometimes the best solution for anxiety is simply to get busy doing something. I was intrigued by a sports writer's interview with Bill Russell a number of years ago. Bill Russell is one of the greatest players in the history of the National Basketball Association, a man who through his defensive prowess dominated his sport and helped bring multiple championships to the Boston Celtics. In this interview, the sports reporter asked the Hall of Famer if he ever got nervous before a game. Russell said, "Before every game, I vomit."[6] That's high anxiety. How did Bill Russell overcome his anxiety? He started the game. Once the game started, the anxiety was gone. Action was the key.

This strategy will also work for us. Sometimes the only way to overcome anxiety is to move into action. At that point, one of two things will happen. If the anxiety had no basis in fact, it will dissolve in the flurry of activity. If the cause for the anxiety was legitimate, we still get some relief because we are at least doing something about it. In either case, action is the key.

Final Word

The Greek word translated "worry" in the newer translations of the New Testament means to draw in different directions, to pull apart, or to distract. That's what anxiety does to us, and that's why we need to develop specific strategies to deal with this major roadblock on the highway of life. Setting aside anxiety will enable us to pull our lives together and enjoy God's peace. Then we can begin once more to enjoy the abundant life Jesus wants us to experience.

Prayer

Lord, forgive us
For worrying instead of worshiping.
For when we worry
Our energies are defused.
But when we worship
Our spirits are renewed.

Forgive us
For leaving you out of
The equation of our lives
And for struggling along
In our own weakness
When we could be infused instead
With your strength.

O Lord, our God
Deliver us
From the distraction
Of our own distractions.

Amen.

NOTES

1 Gary Collins, *Overcoming Anxiety* (Santa Ana CA: Vision House Publishers, 1973), 11.

2 *Quote* 83: 209.

3 Vonette Zachary Bright, *The Greatest Lesson I've Ever Learned* (San Bernardino CA: Here's Life Publishers, 1990), 96-97.

4 Mark Trotter, "Laugh Until It Heals," *Pulpit Digest* (July-August, 1981): 5.

5 George R. Walther, *Power Talking* (New York: Berkley Books, 1991), 119.

6 As recounted in Charles R. Swindoll, *The Grace Awakening* (Dallas: Word Publishing, 1990), 203.

When We're in a Rut

The Boredom Roadblock

A psychologist was making a presentation to the leadership team of a large corporation. He began by describing his experiments with rats. He would put a rat at one end of a maze and a piece of food at the other end. Then he would watch the rat stumble around until he finally found the food. The next time he put the rat in the maze, the rat would stumble around less and find the food faster. After several more times in the maze, the rat would rush through the maze and grab the tidbit of food within a few seconds. Then, the psychologist explained to the group of leaders, he would take the food away. The rat, as before, would make a beeline for the end of the maze, only to discover no food waiting for him. The rat would continue doing this for several more times. Eventually, however, the rat would figure out the food was not going to be there and would stop looking for it. At that point in his discussion, when the psychologist had the attention of the entire seminar group, he presented this dramatic conclusion: "That's the difference between rats and people. The rats stop!"[1]

The psychologist's conclusion caught my attention because it is true. How often do we allow our methods to become ends in themselves? Our routines become ruts. We find ourselves on self-destructive pathways but do not have the courage to change. We do the same things, the same way, at the same time, unable or unwilling to break out of the cycle, bored to distraction by our repeated activity. In such a way, boredom becomes a roadblock that keeps us from being what God wants us to be and enjoying the abundant life Jesus wants us to have. To discover how to navigate around this roadblock on the highway of life, we must turn first to the Scripture.

let

Search the Scripture

As we search the Scriptures, many verses provide guidelines for dealing with the roadblock of boredom. Let me list just a few of them.

- Genesis 12:1: "The LORD had said to Abram, 'Leave your country, your people, and your father's household and go to the land I will show you.'"
- Psalm 34:8: "Taste and see that the LORD is good."
- Proverbs 1:5: "Let the wise listen and add to their learning, and let the discerning get guidance."
- Proverbs 16:22: "Understanding is a fountain of life to those who have it, but folly brings punishment to fools."
- Matthew 10:16: "I am sending you out like sheep among wolves. Therefore be as shrewd as snakes and as innocent as doves."
- Matthew 18:13: "And he said: 'I tell you the truth, unless you change and become like little children, you will never enter the kingdom of heaven.'"
- Luke 5:37-38: "And no one pours new wine into old wineskins. If he does, the new wine will burst the skins, the wine will run out and the wineskins will be ruined. No, new wine must be poured into new wineskins."
- Luke 16:8: "The master commended the dishonest manager because he had acted shrewdly. For the people of this world are more shrewd in dealing with their own kind than are the people of the light."
- 1 Peter 1:13: "Therefore, prepare your minds for action."

These Scriptures reaffirm the necessity of faith in moving around this roadblock. Abraham is a good case in point (Gen 12:1). At the time God told him to leave his home and go to the land of promise, Abraham did not know where he was going, how long he would be gone, or what would happen along the way. God simply told Abraham to go, and he dared to take the step of faith. Faith is not necessarily a leap into the dark, but it is nevertheless a leap. In the words of the psalmist, we need to "taste" before we will know that "the LORD is good" (Ps 34:8). Responding in faith to God's call will break us out of our rut of boredom.

In addition, these Scriptures disclose the importance of wisdom in moving around this roadblock. Several of the passages cited above emphasize the importance of shrewdness in making the leap of faith. Faith does not mean to leap blindly into the dark simply because such a leap will provide an adventure. Wisdom looks at the challenges to go and stretch and think outside the lines and then provides guidelines for our leap of faith. That is why the writer of Proverbs calls for cautious creativity (1:5; 16:22). Learning, discernment, and understanding must accompany the leap of faith.

Likewise, Jesus called for shrewdness in responding to the challenges of life (Matt 10:16; Luke 16:8). On one occasion, for example, Jesus described a servant who was going to lose his job. However, before the termination date, this "unscrupulous" servant altered the accounts of some of his master's customers, hoping they would be helpful to him after he lost his job. When Jesus told this story, the disciples certainly expected Jesus to condemn the unrighteous servant because of his dishonesty. Instead, Jesus had the master of the story praise the unrighteous servant because of his creativity.

Living a creative life of faith does not require placing our brains idly on a shelf. Instead, a life of faith demands the fullest use of our brains. Faith and creativity go hand in hand. Together, they draw us out of our routines and push us toward creative ventures.

The Scriptures also affirm the requirement of change to move around the boredom roadblock. Jesus emphasized this truth in his parable of the wine and wineskins (Luke 5:38). Routines were standard procedure for the religious leaders of Jesus' day. These routines literally squeezed the life out of a person's relationship with God. Jesus called his followers to move past the stifling rules and to get involved in a stimulating relationship with God.

Peter also had in mind this creative kind of thinking in his admonition in 1 Peter 1:13. Peter's image reflected the ancient world when men would "gird up" their long robes around their waists if they needed to run or fight. Peter's challenge to "gird up our minds" is a call to activate our brains. It is a call for creative thinking.

These Scriptures can be sources of help as we try to break out of the ruts in our lives. The Bible is also full of exciting stories of men and women who modeled this kind of creative, risk-taking faith. A woman named Ruth is one of the clearest examples of creativity in the Bible. Let me review the biblical setting for her story.

A Jewish woman named Naomi was married to a man named Elimelech. Because of a famine in the land, this pious Jewish couple and their two sons moved from Palestine to Moab. At this point, Ruth entered the picture. She was a young Moabite woman. The expected response of a young Moabite woman was to marry one of her own kind. Instead, *Ruth broke the pattern* and decided to marry one of the Hebrew sons of Naomi and Elimelech (Ruth 1:4).

After a few years, Elimelech died and both of the sons died. Brokenhearted, Naomi decided to go back home. The expected response of the two daughters-in-law was for them to stay in Moab. Instead, *Ruth broke the pattern.* She decided to attach herself to her mother-in-law and follow her to a strange land (Ruth 1:16-17).

Back in Israel, Ruth and Naomi needed food. The expected response was for them to depend on others in the family to provide for them. Instead, *Ruth broke the pattern.* She chose to take care of the problem herself by gleaning from the fields (Ruth 2:2).

Boaz, a wealthy farmer, noticed Ruth and made sure she was protected as she gleaned the fields. Boaz, as it turned out, was a close relative of her mother-in-law, Naomi. Through a custom called Levirate marriage, it was the responsibility of a close relative to marry the widow of his relative and provide for her. The expected response was for Ruth to sit back and hope this happened. Again, *Ruth broke the pattern.* She opted to take the initiative herself. In collaboration with her mother-in-law, she devised a plan that actually forced the issue (Ruth 3:5). Boaz decided to marry Ruth, and the rest is history.

At each point along the way, Ruth did the unexpected. She refused to get caught in a rut. Instead, at each point, she responded with creativity. She did not follow the trail; she made a trail. She was a model of the creative living that will enable us to break out of our routines.

Set the Strategy

From these Scripture lessons and from the biblical model of Ruth, we can gain both information and inspiration to help us navigate around the roadblock of boredom. And these lessons provide the resources for specific strategies. Let me suggest four.

Strategy #1 is to *challenge the rules*. Of course, life has rules and only the foolish person refuses to follow these rules at all. However, sometimes we expand this "rule" approach to life to such a degree that we get locked into patterns that are no longer applicable to life and our creative juices get squeezed out. Therefore, one way to enhance our creativity is to challenge the rules.

In the movie *IQ*, Walter Matthau played the part of Einstein. Meg Ryan was Einstein's niece. At one point in the movie, Einstein said to his niece, "Question everything!" That's good advice. Every advance in history came from someone who challenged the rules. Columbus discovered America because he challenged the rules of navigation. Martin Luther started the Reformation because he challenged the rules of the church. Einstein discovered the theory of relativity because he challenged the rules of Newtonian physics. Sometimes creativity arises out of the awareness that we do not have to do things in the same way they have always been done.

When we find ourselves in a rut, our first response should be to question everything. Challenging the rules means confronting every activity in our lives with the questions "Why do we have to do it that way?" and "What is a better way to do it?" Challenging the rules will unfetter our creativity.

Strategy #2 is to *reverse the process*. Getting along in this world demands a standard way of understanding the basic phenomena around us. This is what gives order to our lives. However, at times our orderly view of things blinds us to the possibilities around us and locks up our creativity. One way to enhance our creativity is to reverse the way we look at things.

Let me give just one example of how this works. Nineteenth century English physician Edward Jenner used this approach to develop his vaccination for smallpox. He spent years studying people who had smallpox to develop a strategy for dealing with it, to no avail. Finally, he reversed his process. Instead of focusing on people who had smallpox, he focused on people who never had it. He discovered that dairymaids rarely got the disease. It turned out that most dairymaids had had cowpox, a similar but usually nonfatal affliction. Cowpox had vaccinated them against the more dangerous smallpox. This led to Jenner's concept of vaccinating people.[2]

Reversing the process means changing the way we look at things. Reversing the process means approaching our problems from a different perspective. Reversing the process can pull us out of our rut and stimulate our creativity.

Strategy #3 is to *move beyond our borders*. Our minds are bombarded by thousands of bits of information every day. The only way to survive in this kind of world is to focus our mind on specific areas, to narrow the target of our thinking. However, at times our narrow focus of thinking forces us to see things in just one way and locks up our creative machinery. Therefore, one way to enhance our creativity is to think outside our areas.

History is filled with examples of people who have developed innovations in their field from something they learned in other fields. Edwin Drake developed the oil well concept after watching workers drill for salt. He adapted the procedure for getting salt out of the ground to oil, and the modern petroleum industry was born. Roll-on deodorant was an adaptation of the ballpoint pen. Drive-in banks were adapted from drive-in restaurants.[3] The list could go on and on.

Upon finding ourselves in a rut, the right response is to talk to others about what they do in a field totally unrelated to ours, schedule time into our daily schedule for exploring, go someplace we have never been, talk to someone we do not know, or read outside our area of interest or expertise. Getting outside the lines will at times set loose our creativity.

Strategy #4 is to *lighten up*. To be sure, life is a serious matter and therefore we must be careful not to approach it in a frivolous way. However, at times our serious view of life forces us into safe, practical behavior that precludes negative innovation. One of the ways to enhance our creativity is to lighten up, to take a humorous view of life.

How does humor enhance creativity? For one thing, humor relaxes us. Humor is good for both our mental and physical digestion. Humor also forces us to combine ideas that are not usually associated with each other. For example, what do John the Baptist and Winnie the Pooh have in common? The answer: they both have the same middle name. If John the Baptist and Winnie the Pooh can be combined in one thought, what is to keep us from combining other things?

Upon finding ourselves in a rut, the best response is to stop what we are doing and peruse a joke book, watch a comedy program on television, or think of something funny about ourselves. Laugh. Humor has a way of loosening up creativity.

Final Word

Life is too short to go through it in a rut. Staying in our rut will keep us from exploring the side roads that lead to new experiences and unanticipated adventures. Challenging the rules, reversing the process, thinking outside our areas, and sometimes just lightening up will draw us out of our rut. By implementing these strategies, we can navigate around the roadblock of boredom.

Prayer

Creative Father
Who brought everything
Out of nothing
Stir up our creative power.

Help us to see
Not just what is
But also what can be.

Help us to live
Not just out of the past
But also toward the future.

Help us to let go of
What we have made of ourselves
And allow you to make of us
What you want us to be.

Amen.

NOTES

[1] Stephen R. Covey, A. Roger Merrill, and Rebecca R. Merrill, *First Things First* (New York: Simon & Schuster, 1994), 188.

[2] Roger von Oech, *A Whack on the Side of the Head* (New York: Warner Books, 1983), 143-44.

[3] Ibid., 108.

When We Don't Have Time

The Busyness Roadblock

In a *Newsweek* cover story several years back, the writer presented this picture of America today: "We're fried by work, frazzled by lack of time. Technology hasn't made our lives better, just busier. No wonder one-quarter of us say we're exhausted. We need to chill out before we hit the Breaking Point."[1]

Have you ever been there? Are you there now? Fried and frazzled by life, not experiencing a better life, just a busier one? That's an accurate description of life for most of us today. Our lives are controlled by urgent demands that burst into our daily schedules. As a result, we are often exhausted. The Annals of Internal Medicine recently reported that 24 percent of the people surveyed complained of fatigue that lasts longer than two weeks.[2] Fatigue is now among the top five reasons people call the doctor. Perhaps the greatest threat to our health in America today are not cancer, heart attacks, and accidents but calendars, clocks, and telephones. We are killing ourselves with our "busyness."

Our busyness not only leaves us exhausted. It also prevents us from giving attention to our priorities. This preoccupation with the trivial prevents us from focusing on the essential. Consequently, our busyness sidetracks us from the main road that leads to the fulfillment of our lives. Or, to use the terminology we are following in this book, busyness becomes a roadblock that prevents us from experiencing the fullness of life God wants us to have. Therefore, we must find a way to navigate around this roadblock.

Search the Scripture

For the Christian, the place to begin seeking answers is God's word. Several Scriptures provide insight to help us move around the roadblock of busyness. Let me list some of them.

- Psalm 25:5: "Lead me in Thy truth and teach me, for Thou art the God of my salvation; for Thee I wait all the day" (KJV).
- Psalm 27:14: "Wait for the LORD; be strong and take heart and wait for the LORD."
- Psalm 37:7: "Be still before the LORD and wait patiently for him; do not fret when men succeed in their ways, when they carry out their wicked schemes."
- Psalm 90:12: "Teach us to number our days aright, that we may gain a heart of wisdom."
- Ecclesiastes 2:4-6, 11: "I undertook great projects: I built houses for myself and planted vineyards. I made gardens and parks and planted all kinds of fruit trees in them. I made reservoirs to water groves of flourishing trees. . . Yet when I surveyed all that my hands had done and what I had toiled to achieve, everything was meaningless, a chasing after the wind; nothing was gained under the sun."
- Isaiah 5:11-12: "Woe to those who rise early in the morning to run after their drinks, who stay up late at night till they are inflamed with wine. They have harps and lyres at their banquets, tambourines and flutes and wine, but they have no regard for the deeds of the LORD, no respect for the work of his hands."
- Isaiah 40:31: "Yet those who wait for the LORD will gain new strength; they will mount up with wings like eagles, they will run and not get tired, they will walk and not become weary."
- Mark 6:31: Jesus said, "Come with me by yourselves to a quiet place and get some rest." Mark added this note of explanation: "So many people were coming and going that they did not even have a chance to eat."

These Scriptures remind us, first of all, of the danger of our busyness. Sometimes, when we are too busy, we move ahead of God and thus out of relationship with him. But since our strength comes from our relationship with the Lord, when we break that relationship, we lose our strength for facing the challenges of life. Being too busy is a dangerous thing (Isa 5:11-12; 40:31).

Michele McCormick articulated this danger in an editorial titled "We're Too Busy for Ideas." The busyness of our time, Michele suggests, has robbed us of the opportunity for quiet reflection that is essential to our success in public and private life. We are simply too busy to think. What do we miss when we fail to set aside time to think? Michele answered that question like this: "The best ideas occur to me when my mind is otherwise unchallenged and there is no pressure to create. I have mentally composed whole articles while jogging, flashed upon the solution to a software dilemma while sitting in the steam room, come up with just the right opening line for a client's speech while pushing a vacuum. These were not problems I had set out to address at those particular times. Inventiveness came to my uncluttered mind in a random, unfocused moment."[3] Being too busy to think is a dangerous thing.

In addition, these Scriptures reflect on one of the reasons for our busyness. Afraid that someone else will get more than we do, we are often captivated by the craving for the things of this world (Ps 37:7; Isa 5:11-12). As the old quip puts it, "We spend money we don't have to buy things we don't need based on advertising we don't believe to please people we don't even like."

Author Juliet B. Schor describes the problem in terms of today's consumer society. She locates the problem in what she calls the process of consumption: see, want, borrow, and buy. Our inner desires are prompted by exposure to a plethora of things. Seeing leads to wanting, as our inner desires spur us to action. And often we do not wait until we have the money we need before we purchase something. We simply charge it. Then, after having bought something—often on credit—we are driven to make more money to cover what we have already purchased, all the time driven toward more possessions by the process of consumption.[4]

In addition, these Scriptures remind us of the result of our busyness. The writer of Ecclesiastes testifies that in his day, as in our day, the accumulation of material possessions does not bring meaning and purpose to life (Eccl 2:4-6, 11). Henri Nouwen's term—"an illusion of immortality"—describes the pattern many of us fall into today. We keep giving eternal value to the things we own and to the people we know and to the plans we have and to the successes we collect.[5] But the things of this world are not immortal; they are temporary. I noticed a bumper sticker the other day that read, "Whoever has the most toys when he dies is still dead!" If things become the foundation of our lives, someday we are in for a big fall.

Finally, these Scriptures teach us the antidote for our busyness. We see this particularly in Jesus' admonition to "Come with me by yourselves to a quiet place and get some rest" (Matt 6:31). Jesus acknowledged the need for times of rest and recreation, because without these times of spiritual, emotional, physical, and mental rest and recreation, the roadblock called busyness will block our pathway toward the abundant life Jesus wants us to enjoy.

The proper way to deal with busyness is not only reflected in individual Scriptures like the ones cited above but also in individuals who modeled the proper response to busyness in their own lives. One of the most intriguing biblical examples of someone who understood the plight of busyness and suggested a viable alternative to it was Jethro, the father-in-law of Moses (Exod 18). Jethro is not one of the official heroes of the Bible. However, had Jethro not stepped in at a crucial time, we might have never heard of one of the true heroes of the Bible—Moses. In fact, humanly speaking, we could say that Jethro made Moses what he was. Let me tell you how he did that.

Moses was the leader of the Hebrew people, and he also made judgments about all the issues troubling his people. As a result, the Hebrew people stood around Moses from morning until evening, each waiting his turn to speak to Moses. Jethro, who was Moses' father-in-law, asked Moses, "What is this thing that you are doing for the people?" (Exod 18:14). Moses answered, "Because the people come to me to inquire of God" (Exod 18:15). In other words, Moses said, "I'm doing it because I am their leader and they expect me to solve all their problems." Instead of being impressed, Jethro responded, "The thing you are doing is not good" (Exod 18:17). Then Jethro explained why it was not good: "You will surely wear out, both yourself and these people who are with you, for the task is too heavy for you; you cannot do it alone" (Exod 18:18). Now that he had Moses' attention, Jethro offered a solution to the problem. "You shall select out of all the people able men who fear God, men of truth, those who hate dishonest gain; and you shall place them over them, as leaders of thousands, of hundreds, of fifties and of tens" (Exod 18:21).

Moses was too busy because he was trying to do everything himself. That is, he was using the wrong method to accomplish a worthwhile goal. Jethro suggested a plan that enabled Moses to move around the roadblock of busyness and yet still accomplish his goal. And Moses did what Jethro said. We'll flesh out Jethro's suggestion as we outline our strategy.

Set the Strategy

These Scriptures and Jethro's model provide resources out of which to develop specific strategies for steering around the roadblock of busyness.

Strategy #1 is to *evaluate.* The beginning point in dealing with our busy schedules is to evaluate our actions. This process of evaluation begins with *our value system.* Focusing on our value systems reveals the "why" of our actions. In many cases, we discover that our busyness comes from trying to live by a value system to which we should not be committed in the first place. Our focus is wrongly directed to personal preferences instead of to kingdom priorities. Next, the process of evaluation should focus on *our goals* and identify "what" we want to accomplish. It is not enough to get to the top of the ladder. The ladder must be leaning against the right wall. Therefore, after determining that our goals are worthy of our time, we need to make sure our actions will move us toward the achievement of those goals. Then our evaluation should focus on *our methods.* This deals with the "how" of our actions. The ends never justify the means. Instead, our methods must be congruent with our value system and with our ultimate goals.

Having evaluated our actions, we should next give our attention to *how we use our discretionary time.* Most of us have four kinds of time: superior time (time controlled by our boss); peer time (time required by those with whom we work); subordinate time (time demanded by those who work for us); and discretionary time (time that is in our control). Much of our time is not under our control, but some of it is. Determining the best way to use that time is a key part of the evaluation process.

Evaluating how we use our discretionary time will bring us face to face with *our time wasters.* Time management expert Alec Mackenzie lists these as among the top time wasters: telephone, visitors, unnecessary meetings, paperwork, management by crisis, and lack of planning.[6] Each of us has our own list. After developing our personal lists, we must target each time waster with a specific strategy.

Before we can do something about our busyness, we must first understand why we are so busy. That understanding comes through constant evaluation. So the first strategy in response to busyness is to determine what we are doing and why and how.

Strategy #2 is to *eliminate.* Evaluation provides the data for the second strategy: elimination of inessential obligations. Perhaps the most important factor in unraveling the busyness of our lives is the courage to say no to the things that are not really important so we can say yes to the things that are. For most of us, the problem is not that we don't know what to do but that we don't know what not to do. Eliminating the inessentials from our lives is crucial.

Bobby Richardson, a former New York Yankee, demonstrated this strategy. He was thirty years old and at the height of his career for the Yankees. Del Webb, the Yankees co-owner, pushed a blank contract across the table and asked Richardson to fill it in. Bobby pushed it back across the table, saying, "The Yankees have treated me well, and I am not interested in filling in the blanks in that contract. My interest is filling in the blanks in my life as a husband and a father. My last game was my last game."[7] Bobby had a blank contract in front of him. However, instead of signing on the dotted line, he decided to get on with his life. He had the courage to eliminate what was not important so he could give himself to what was important. Bobby Richardson demonstrated the second strategy in response to busyness: eliminating the inessential.

Strategy #3 is to *delegate.* After eliminating unnecessary things, much remains to be done, usually too much for any one person to do. The third strategy is to delegate. The same *Newsweek* article cited at the beginning of the chapter contains the story of former Harvard President Neil Rudenstine. During the first period of his administration, he approached his job with a mania for detail. His basic work style could be described with the word "obsession." After three years of intensive nonstop hyperactivity, Rudenstine hit the wall. He took a three-month sabbatical. Then, when he returned to his post, he promised to delegate more and obsess less.[8]

What Rudenstine did in our day, Jethro urged Moses to do about three millennia ago. Moses did not need to work harder; he needed to work smarter. He needed to delegate. In Moses' day and in ours, delegation is based on two principles. Principle one: no person can do everything. Hence,

Moses had to let go of some of his responsibility. And principle two: other people are competent. Hence, Moses had to depend on others to carry out the responsibility he gave to them. Sharing the load allows each of us to have breathing room. The third strategy in response to busyness, then, is to delegate to others the tasks they can legitimately and effectively accomplish.

Strategy #4 is to *orchestrate*. After evaluating our actions, eliminating the inessential, and delegating what someone else can do, a full agenda may still stare us in the face. The strategy at this point is effective planning. Some might complain, "I don't have time to plan." In reality, we don't have time not to plan. If busyness is a roadblock for us, we need to develop a systematic plan that will enable us to carry out our activities effectively. All good plans must distinguish between priorities—those things that have to be done—and posteriorities—those things that are inconsequential. All good plans must include both a destination—understanding clearly our ultimate goal—and a route plan—understanding how we will get there. And all good plans must include a time schedule—when will each part of the plan be implemented—and a cost schedule—what will each step along the way cost. Orchestrating our lives with the same care with which we plan our summer vacations is the final strategy in moving around the roadblock called busyness.

Final Word

Many years ago churchman D. T. Niles said, "Hurry means that we gather impressions but have no experiences. We collect acquaintances but make no friends. We attend meetings but experience no encounters with God."[9] That is no way to live. To experience real life we are going to have to deal with this roadblock called "busyness." Only then can we enjoy the abundant life Jesus wants us to experience.

Prayer

O God,
Forgive us
For our abuse of time.
We mistake activity
For productivity

And motion
For meaning
We seem to be
Making good time
But we've forgotten
Where we're going
And why

O Lord, our God
Slow us down
So we can hear again
Your still, small voice.

Amen.

NOTES

[1] *Newsweek* (6 March 1995): 56.

[2] Ibid., 58.

[3] *Newsweek* (29 March 1993): 10.

[4] Juliet B. Schor, *The Overspent American* (New York: Basic Books, 1998), 68-74.

[5] Jurjen Beumer, *Henri Nouwen: A Restless Seeking for God* (New York: The Crossroad Publishing Company, 1997), 95.

[6] R. Alec Mackenzie, *The Time Trap* (New York: McGraw-Hill Book Company, 1972), 86.

[7] Yogi Berra with Tom Horton, *Yogi: It Ain't Over . . .* (New York: Harper & Row, 1989), 43.

[8] *Newsweek* (6 March 1995): 57-58.

[9] Andrew W. Blackwood, *The Growing Minister* (Grand Rapids MI: Baker Book House, 1960), 127.

When We Can't Say What We Really Mean

The Communication Roadblock

Sometimes changing the location of a single word in a sentence dramatically changes the meaning of the sentence. Let me illustrate. Consider the following sentence: "I hit him in the eye yesterday." This is a simple sentence. But by inserting the word "only" at different places in the sentence, we can totally change the meaning. *"Only* I hit him in the eye yesterday." Not everybody hit him. I was the only one who hit him. "I *only* hit him in the eye yesterday." I didn't poke his eye out. I only hit him there. "I hit *only* him in the eye yesterday." I didn't hit everyone in the eye, only him. "I hit him *only* in the eye yesterday." I did not hit him all over his body, only in the eye. "I hit him in the *only* eye yesterday." He had one good eye and that's the eye I hit. "I hit him in the eye *only* yesterday." Not every day this week, but just yesterday I hit him.

This exercise clearly demonstrates the complexity of communication and reminds us of the importance of every word that comes out of our mouths. What a person says, how he says it, and sometimes what a person doesn't say all communicate to others. And the effectiveness of our communication determines the level of our achievement. Effective communication enables us to achieve our goals. On the other hand, ineffective communication leaves us stumbling from one fiasco to another. Consequently, ineffective communication is another roadblock that will keep us from being what God wants us to be and from doing what God wants us to do. We must therefore learn how to pilot our lives around this roadblock.

Search the Scripture

For the Christian, the place to begin seeking answers is within God's word. Many Scriptures in both the Old Testament and the New Testament reflect on this roadblock. Let me cite some of the most helpful ones.

- Psalm 19:14: "May the words of my mouth and the meditation of my heart be pleasing in your sight, O LORD, my Rock and my Redeemer."
- Psalm 141:3: "Set a guard over my mouth, O LORD; keep watch over the door of my lips."
- Proverbs 4:1: "Listen and grow wise" (TLB).
- Proverbs 15:23: "Everyone enjoys giving good advice, and how wonderful it is to be able to say the right thing at the right time!" (TLB).
- Proverbs 25:11: "A word aptly spoken is like apples of gold in settings of silver."
- Ecclesiastes 10:12: "Words from a wise man's mouth are gracious, but a fool is consumed by his own lips."
- Matthew 5:37: "Simply let your 'Yes' be 'Yes,' and your 'No,' 'No'; anything beyond this comes from the evil one."
- Matthew 12:36: "But I tell you that men will have to give account on the day of judgment for every careless word they have spoken."
- Ephesians 4:29: "Do not let any unwholesome talk come out of your mouths, but only what is helpful for building others up according to their needs, that it may benefit those who listen."
- James 3:7-8: "All kinds of animals, birds, reptiles and creatures of the sea are being tamed and have been tamed by man, but no man can tame the tongue. It is a restless evil, full of deadly poison."

These Scriptures remind us of our accountability for the way we communicate. We can honor God with our words, and we can dishonor God with our words. But in either case, we are responsible for these words. Jesus reminds us that we will eventually give an account to God for every word we speak (Matt 12:36).

Accountability is a good news/bad news kind of thing. The bad news is that accountability places the responsibility squarely on our shoulders for every word that comes out of our mouths. We cannot escape the responsibility for our words. On the other hand, the good news is that accountability places the ability with us to make good choices. We cannot escape the responsibility for our words, but we can control our words. Paul acknowledged our ability to control our communication in his admonition to the Ephesian Christians (Eph 4:29).

These Scriptures also illustrate the difficulty of communication. The psalmist acknowledged the difficulty of controlling our communication without the direct intervention of God (Ps 141:3), a thought echoed in James 3. The writer of Proverbs affirmed that communication consists not only of speaking but also of listening, thus adding to the complexity of the process (Prov 4:1). Further, the writer of Proverbs declared that communication is not just a matter of saying the right thing. It is a matter of saying the right thing at the right time (15:23; 25:11). This thought is not meant to encourage dishonesty. It simply suggests sensitivity to others. And the writer of Ecclesiastes noted the fine line between words that reflect our grace and words that reflect our shame (Eccl 10:12). When I heard this word from the wise man who wrote Ecclesiastes, I was reminded of an old wag who says, "Better to remain silent and be thought a fool than to speak up and remove all doubt." Communication is a complex, difficult challenge.

At the same time, these Scriptures affirm the importance of communication. Jesus called for simplicity and directness in our communication. More than that, he called for honesty. A loose translation of Jesus' statement is "Say what you mean and mean what you say" (Matt 5:37). Paul's word to the Ephesians (Eph 4:29) is replete with suggestions for the Christian. We are reminded of the need for communication that is clean, appropriate, encouraging, and positive, for such communication creates an environment for cooperation and achievement.

Writer Frederick Buechner has done as much as anyone else in our generation to illustrate the importance of communication, not only in the way he writes but also in what he says. In one of his autobiographical works, he reveals the time in class when he first became aware of the importance of communication. The teacher's name was Mr. Martin. Buechner explains, "Through him I started to sense that words not only convey something, but are something; that words have color, depth, texture of their own, and the power to evoke vastly more than they mean; that words can be used not merely to make things clear, make things vivid, make things interesting and whatever else, but to make things happen inside the one who reads them or hears them."[1] Because of the power of words, how we use words is extremely important.

Scripture teaches us through its precepts but also through the personalities who inhabit the pages of the Bible. One of the most amazing models of effective communication skills in the Bible was the man named Nehemiah. While in captivity, Nehemiah received word about conditions back in Judah. He returned to Jerusalem and, against tremendous opposition, led the citizens in rebuilding the walls of the city, a task they completed in just fifty-two days (Neh 6:15).

From a divine standpoint, Nehemiah and his contemporaries completed this incredible task because of God's empowerment. Nehemiah 6:16 says, "When all our enemies heard about this, all the surrounding nations were afraid and lost their self-confidence, because they realized that this work had been done with the help of our God." However, from a human perspective, the key to Nehemiah's success was his communication skills.

Nehemiah's communication skills that enabled him to complete the task are clearly demonstrated throughout the story. The story begins with Nehemiah in communication with God (Neh 1:5-11). Before talking to the king, Nehemiah talked to God. Then Nehemiah communicated his concern to King Artaxerxes. So effective was he in communicating his desire that King Artaxerxes not only allowed him to return home. He also sent letters authorizing Nehemiah to pass safely through all the surrounding countries. The king even provided the material Nehemiah needed to complete his task (2:1-8). After returning to Jerusalem, Nehemiah inspected the walls of the city. He then communicated to the local citizens the need to rebuild the walls. So effective was his communication that the majority of the people joined him in this effort (2:17-20). Apparently, then, Nehemiah's communication skills enabled his helpers to overcome both outward criticism (ch. 4) and inward corruption (ch. 5). Through effective communication, Nehemiah kept the workers going in the midst of the plot of Sanballat and Tobiah (ch. 6). Victory came not only because of the power of God, but also because of the words of Nehemiah. He is a model of what we are talking about in this chapter. Studying his life will teach us further lessons about communication.

Set the Strategy

However, we need more than an example and a few Scriptures to get us around this roadblock. We also need to translate the example and develop scriptural admonitions into practical strategies. Let me suggest a few of these strategies.

Strategy #1 is to *learn how to listen empathetically.* Steven Covey defines "empathetic listening" as "listening with the intent to understand."[2] Perhaps the greatest barrier to effective communication is the unwillingness to listen, and the greatest aid to effective communication is empathetic listening. To listen empathetically means to *concentrate.* People speak an average of 125-140 words per minute, but our minds think from 400-500 words per minute. Consequently, it takes great concentration to keep our minds on what another person is saying. To listen empathetically also means to *care.* Instead of listening to others, most of us use the time while they speak to formulate our response. In contrast, caring about what others say enough to concentrate on what they are saying will enable us to become good listeners. And better listening will lead to more effective communication.

Strategy #2 is to *develop our relationships.* Sometimes the barrier to our communication with other people is not our inability to listen or our lack of communication skills but rather a relationship tension between us and the other person. It might be a low trust level, unmet expectations, hurt feelings, unresolved conflict, or one of a dozen other relationship problems. If these tensions in our relationship are the barrier to our communication, then improving the relationship can enhance the communication. The status of our relationships can make or break communication. Tension in our relationships can deter communication. But when the relationship is strong, communication flows freely.

Strategy #3 is to *participate in face-to-face dialogues.* The communication process is also enhanced by dialogue carried out by two people who are face to face with each other. Face-to-face dialogue is the most effective means of communicating for several reasons. For starters, our presence is more arresting than a long distance communication and not as easily ignored. Also, in face-to-face dialogue, fewer things can interfere with the communication process. Further, being face-to-face with another person allows immediate feedback so that the conversation can move to a deeper level, for the immediate feedback allows instant corrections and clarifications. Therefore, the best communication is not done via a note or e-mail. The best communication takes place when two people sit down with each other and look into each other's eyes as they dialogue. Effective communication requires committing ourselves to frequent face-to-face dialogues.

Strategy #4 is to *be sensitive to nonverbal clues.* Since nonverbal factors account for 93 percent of communication according to most communication experts, being sensitive to nonverbal clues is vital to the process of communication. The call to be sensitive to nonverbal clues applies to our listening as well as to our speaking. On the one hand, the process of listening involves more than hearing words. Effective listeners read the other person's eyes, note the expression on the other person's face, remember the context out of which the other person speaks, and discern what is in the other person's heart. On the other hand, the process of speaking also involves more than our words. The inflection of our words, the expression on our faces, our posture, how we hold our hands, and whether or not we look at the person to whom we are speaking—all of these nonverbal factors communicate. Effective communicators not only watch what they say. They also are concerned by how they say it. They are cued in to nonverbal clues. If our words say one thing but our body language says something else, people are more likely to believe our body language.

Final Word

Communication is not easy. Instead, communication is one of life's greatest challenges and also one of life's greatest achievements. Communication enables us to express our thoughts. Communication also enables us to create community. Eugene Peterson encompasses both of these dimensions as he describes two distinct kinds of words: "In a kind of rough-and-ready sorting out, most words can be set in one of two piles: words for communion and words for communication. Words for communion are used to tell stories, make love, nurture intimacies, and develop trust. Words for communication are used to buy stocks, sell cauliflower, direct traffic, and teach algebra. Both piles of words are necessary."[3] Indeed they are. That's why the more effectively we communicate, the more effectively we will be able to move from where we are to where God wants us to be.

Prayer

Dear Lord,
How often we
Speak without thinking
Or even worse
Speak what we are thinking
When our thinking is askew.

We forget that our words
Not only are something
But also do something.

We forget that
Worse than sticks and stones
Our words can hurt others.

Help us to learn how
To speak the truth
In love
So that our words
Can become
Acceptable in your sight
And helpful to your kingdom

Amen.

NOTES

[1] Frederick Buechner, *The Sacred Journey* (San Francisco: Harper & Row, 1982), 68.

[2] Stephen R. Covey, *The Seven Habits of Highly Effective People* (New York: Simon and Schuster, 1989), 248.

[3] Eugene H. Peterson, *Under the Unpredictable Plant* (Grand Rapids MI: William B. Eerdmans Publishing Company, 1992), 191.

When Others Don't Like What We Do

The Criticism Roadblock

Bud Wilkinson, while coaching the Oklahoma Sooners, set a mark that will probably never be eclipsed by any other college football coach. He led his team to forty-seven straight victories. Following the victory over Texas on October 10, 1953, the Oklahoma Sooners would not be beaten or tied until November 16, 1957, forty-seven games later. Playing against Notre Dame on that Saturday afternoon in 1957, the winning streak finally came to an end with a 7-0 loss to the Irishmen. Some of you are probably not particularly interested in football nostalgia, but here's why I'm recalling this piece of gridiron history. As the Oklahoma fans left the stadium, two of the Oklahoma supporters were overheard saying, "Wilkinson hasn't got it anymore. He's been around too long!"[1] If people didn't like what Coach Wilkinson was doing when his team won forty-seven straight football games, they are certainly not going to like everything we do.

That is a fact of life. No one escapes criticism. The difference between people is not that some people are criticized and others are not. The difference is that some people are stimulated by criticism and others are stopped by it. On the one hand, criticism can stimulate us to higher achievement. On the other hand, criticism can become a roadblock that prevents us from experiencing the full and abundant life God wants us to have. Consequently, each of us must determine how to plot a course around the roadblock of criticism.

We will respond t. Criticism

Search the Scripture

For the Christian, the place to begin seeking answers is God's Word. And the Bible repeatedly speaks to the issue of criticism. Note the following examples.

- Psalm 102:8: "My enemies have reproached me all day long; those who deride me have used my name as a curse."
- Proverbs 11:11: "Through the blessing of the upright a city is exalted, but by the mouth of the wicked it is destroyed.
- Proverbs 23:12: "Don't refuse to accept criticism; get all the help you can" (TLB).
- Proverbs 28:13: "A man who refuses to admit his mistakes can never be successful. But if he confesses and forsakes them, he gets another chance" (TLB).
- Matthew 7:1: "Jesus warned, 'Do not judge lest you be judged. For in the way you judge, you will be judged; and by your standard of measure, it will be measured to you.'"
- Romans 14:10: "But you, why do you judge your brother? Or you again, why do you regard your brother with contempt? For we shall all stand before the judgment seat of God."
- Romans 14:13: "Let us therefore stop turning critical eyes on one another. If we must be critical, let us be critical of our own conduct and see that we do nothing to make a brother stumble or fall" (Phillips).
- Ephesians 4:29: "Do not let any unwholesome talk come out of your mouths, but only what is helpful for building others up according to their needs, that it may benefit those who listen."
- James 4:11: "Brothers, do not slander one another. Anyone who speaks against his brother or judges him speaks against the law and judges it."

These Scriptures affirm that criticism is universal. Criticism is not our exclusive lot but rather it is the universal experience of humanity (Ps 102:8).

Criticism plagued Moses and the prophets and Paul—all great people of faith. Even Jesus was criticized. Likewise, down through history, the greatest of God's saints have experienced criticism. So when people criticize us, that puts us in good company. It takes neither brains nor talent nor character to get started in the business of grumbling. Yet, many people chose that vocation and as a result the world never has a shortage of critics.

Further, these Scriptures suggest that at times criticism can be helpful. Criticism is not always bad. Sometimes criticism is good because it ferrets out a faulty action or attitude on our part that needs to be corrected. For example, the writer of Proverbs wisely suggested the need to listen to criticism and learn from it rather than to automatically reject it (23:12; Pr 28:13).

On the other hand, these Scriptures also acknowledge that criticism can at times be harmful. The writer of Proverbs experienced the destructive force of criticism (11:11). In early American history, Thomas Jefferson was almost ruined by criticism. Thomas Jefferson was governor of Virginia at the time. The British invaded the colony of Virginia and wreaked havoc throughout the countryside before withdrawing. Jefferson was accused of negligence and had to undergo a review of the state legislature. Even though he was eventually exonerated, he nevertheless felt the pain of being accused before his peers. He later said, "I find the pain of a little censure, even when it is unfounded, is more acute than the pleasure of much praise."[2]

Criticism can be devastating in its effect, whether it is deserved or not. That's why the New Testament repeatedly concludes that criticism is not an acceptable part of the lifestyle of the Christian (Matt 7:1; Rom 14:10; Rom 14:13). Instead of tearing down other people through criticism, Christians are to build up other people through encouragement. In so doing, Christians follow the royal law of God, which is love (Jas 2:8).

Finally, these Scriptures remind us that criticism is contagious. Life operates under the echo principle, by and large. Consequently, what we send out comes back to us and thus our words can return to haunt us, and our actions can stimulate patterns in others that often boomerang back to us. That was Jesus' point in Matthew 7:1. Jesus was not suggesting that our criticism of someone for a certain act will cause them to criticize us for that same act. Instead, he was explaining that when we hold other people to impossible standards, they will in turn hold us to impossible standards. A critical spirit begets critical spirits.

Each of these Scriptures provides helpful hints on how to move around the roadblock of criticism. We can learn further lessons from a sterling Old Testament character who modeled the proper response to criticism. His name was Jeremiah. The prophet Jeremiah was one of the most criticized people in the Bible, apart from the Lord Christ himself. Jeremiah describes this criticism in Jeremiah 20:10-11: "I hear many whispering, 'Terror on every side! Report him! Let's report him!' All my friends are waiting for me to slip, saying, 'Perhaps he will be deceived; then we will prevail over him and take our revenge on him.'"

Jeremiah demonstrated an appropriate response to criticism. He responded first with *despair*. "Why does the way of the wicked prosper?" Jeremiah complained. "Why do all the faithless live at ease?" (12:1). That is a common reaction to criticism initially. Then, Jeremiah moved from despair to *a desire for revenge*. "Drag them off like sheep to be butchered!" Jeremiah demanded. "Set them apart for the day of slaughter!" (12:3). Again, this is a natural part of the process through which we evolve when someone criticizes us. But it cannot be the final step, and it was not for Jeremiah. Eventually, Jeremiah responded to his criticism with *the hope that God would set things right*. We see this final stage in 20:11: "But the LORD is with me like a dread champion; therefore my persecutors will stumble and not prevail." And again in verse 13: "Sing to the LORD, praise the LORD! For he has delivered the soul of the needy one from the hand of evildoers."

Like Jeremiah, each of us will receive criticism. Jeremiah provides a realistic pattern of response. After the initial despair and desire for revenge, Jeremiah came to the position of hope that God would eventually set things right. Our response to criticism should move us through those same three steps.

Set the Strategy

These Scriptural lessons and the example of Jeremiah provide resources from which we can develop our strategies for navigating around the roadblock of criticism. Let me sketch out some strategies that will help.

Strategy #1 is *realization*. A rather pugnacious elderly lady took the witness stand. The young attorney, full of himself, marched up to her and asked, "Do you know me?" "Of course I know you," she retorted. "You're a crook. You've been a crook ever since you stole the washing off my line as a little boy, and you're a crook now!" The young lawyer was stunned, but came back with a second question, "Do you know the attorney there on the opposing side?" The lady responded, "Of course, I know him! He's a bigger crook than you are! He's been a crook ever since he shot the street lights out in front of my house, and he's an even bigger crook now." About that time, the judge, who had also grown up in that town, leaned forward and admonished the young attorney, "If you ask her if she knows me, I'm going to hold you in contempt of court!"

The judge is right. When someone gets to know us, they can quickly spot something to criticize, for no one is perfect. As a result, criticism is going to come to all of us. The first step in moving around the roadblock of criticism is the realization that criticism will inevitably come. Without coming to that realization, most of us will end up having our own little pity party.

Strategy #2 is *evaluation*. Accepting the inevitability of criticism frees us to evaluate criticism objectively. Evaluation is facilitated when we categorize the criticisms directed toward us. Some criticism has no basis in fact. That is category one. This criticism comes not because something is wrong with us but because something is wrong with the person who criticizes us. For example, one of Erma Bombeck's college professors told her she had no talent in writing. "Don't even try it!" was his critical advice.[3] He was obviously wrong, and Erma Bombeck fortunately ignored his criticism. Likewise, some of the criticism directed at us is misguided.

Other criticism directed toward us is precisely true. That is category two. We are often tempted to assume that all criticism fits into category one and therefore summarily dismiss all criticism with a defensive spirit. Defensiveness is based on the assumption that we are beyond reproach and that all criticism must therefore be false. Such is not the case, of course. We must therefore acknowledge this second category of criticism. Some criticism is right on target. We are guilty as charged. Admission of our culpability will free us to begin planning how we can correct the problem that generated the criticism.

But not all criticism fits neatly into these two categories—completely false on the one hand or completely true on the other. We must also acknowledge a third category. Some criticism is partially true and partially false. In such cases, the proper response is to ignore the part that is invalid without also rejecting the part that is valid. Categorizing criticism is an essential step in determining the proper response to it.

Strategy #3 is *contemplation*. At this point, categorization should give way to contemplation. Strategy #3 is to contemplate what can be done about the criticism, legitimate and illegitimate, that has been directed toward us. If the criticism is valid or partially accurate, the proper response is to determine what we can do to address the problem. An old saying is probably accurate: "Most of us would rather be ruined by praise than saved by criticism." But with the proper response, some criticism can actually help us.

For example, when I was pastor of a church in Pensacola, I received a letter from a lady who was known for her outspokenness. When I realized it was from her, my first temptation was to toss it into the trashcan. Instead, I decided to read it. This critic reminded me that her mother was in the nursing home, and she criticized me and the staff for not visiting her mother on a regular basis. The criticism, in this case, was accurate. The staff did not have a plan for visiting our shut-ins, a failure that this lady correctly identified. So instead of becoming defensive, our staff developed a plan that enabled us during the rest of my ministry there to take care of this problem, a plan that would never have developed had we not honestly evaluated the criticism. To valid criticism, the proper response is corrective action.

On the other hand, if the criticism is invalid, the best response is to forget it. Let me illustrate. A young man asked his older friend what he should do in response to a newspaper article in which he was slandered. The older adviser said, "Do nothing. Half of the people who bought the paper didn't see the article. Half of the people who saw the article didn't read it. Half of the people who read the article didn't believe it. Half of the people who believed it don't amount to anything anyway. Forget it." When criticism is not valid, the proper response is to allow it to go in one ear and out the other.

But let me add the precaution I noted above. Avoid the danger of automatically rejecting all criticism with the assumption that it is invalid. Often it is not. Often the criticism is right on target. The best strategy is to evaluate the criticism honestly, spend time thinking about it, and then determine which criticism is to be ignored and which is to be acknowledged.

Strategy #4 is *activation*. After we have categorized the criticism and found it to be valid, after we have contemplated the criticism and determined the appropriate response, then we need to act. In his book *Six Action Shoes*, author Edward de Bono invents a word we need to appropriate into our personal vocabulary in response to criticism. It is the word "operacy,"

To take slip & 55 +.
cha_.

which is the skill of action. If the criticism reminds us of something lacking in our lives, operacy will motivate us to begin doing this thing. If the criticism reminds us of something that should not be present in our lives, operacy will motivate us to stop doing this thing. Evaluation and contemplation are worth nothing unless they lead to action.[4]

take slip to Closed

Final Word

A well-known preacher of the past prayed for holy numbness. That is often our prayer, but it should not always be our prayer. Sometimes our prayer should be for holy sensitivity that will enable us to recognize the criticism directed toward us, enable us to evaluate the criticism honesty, force us to face up to what must be done, and then mobilize us into action. Only then can criticism become a stepping-stone to higher accomplishment rather than a roadblock that prevents us from enjoying the abundant life Jesus wants us to experience.

Prayer

Dear Father
Judge of all people
Remind us of
Our accountability to you.

In your eyes,
We stand condemned
Because of our sin.
Help us to acknowledge that.

In your eyes,
We stand accepted
Because of your grace.
Help us to affirm that.

Let us find peace
In your acceptance.
And help us to be
Accepting of others
In your peace.

Amen.

NOTES

[1] Jay Wilkinson with Gretchen Hirsch, *Bud Wilkinson* (Champaign IL: Sagamore Publishing, 1994), 66.

[2] Saul K. Padover, *Jefferson* (New York: Mentor, 1970), 54-55.

[3] Susan Edwards, *Erma Bombeck: A Life in Humor* (New York: Avon Books, 1997), 44.

[4] Edward de Bono, *Six Actions Shoes* (New York: HarperBusiness, 1991), ix.

When We Feel Boxed In

The Depression Roadblock

Dr. Nathan Kline, physician and medical researcher, calls it the common cold of psychiatric ills.[1] The Medieval physicians referred to it as melancholy. The common name for it is depression. Whatever you call it, depression is another roadblock that keeps us from becoming what God wants us to become and doing what God wants us to do.

Depression comes from four basic sources. Some depression springs from *biological causes.* Low blood sugar, hormonal deficiencies, an imbalance in our electrolytes, and even fatigue are a few of the biological causes of depression. On other occasions, *sociological causes* are at the root of our depression. Either in the environment in which we grew up or in the social context in which we now live, the absence of ego support can create fertile soil for the development of depression. *Psychological causes* also contribute to our depression. Many of us respond to the failures of our lives with self-blame or self-pity. Either pathway leads eventually to depression. Finally, depression can be created by or fed by *spiritual causes.* We sin against God and our guilt leads to depression.

The biological, sociological, psychological, and spiritual circumstances of our lives provide the seedbed for depression. And depression blocks us from being what God wants us to be and enjoying the abundant life he wants us to experience. It is another roadblock on the highway of life for many people.

Search the Scripture

For the Christian, the place to begin seeking answers is within God's word. Many Scriptures speak words of challenge and encouragement to those who suffer from depression. Let me list a few of these.

- Psalm 30:5: "Weeping may remain for a night, but rejoicing comes in the morning."
- Psalm 31:24: "Be strong and take heart, all you who hope in the LORD."
- Isaiah 43:2-3: "When you pass through the waters, I will be with you; and when you pass through the rivers, they will not sweep over you. When you walk through the fire, you will not be burned; the flames will not set you ablaze. For I am the LORD, your God, the Holy One of Israel, your Savior."
- Matthew 11:28: "Come to me, all of you who are weary and overburdened, and I will give you rest!" (Phillips).
- Luke 18:1: "Then Jesus told his disciples a parable to show them that they should always pray and not give up."
- Romans 8:18: "I consider that our present sufferings are not worth comparing with the glory that will be revealed in us."
- 2 Corinthians 4:8-10: "We are hard pressed on every side, but not crushed; perplexed, but not in despair; persecuted, but not abandoned; struck down, but not destroyed. We always carry around in our body the death of Jesus, so that the life of Jesus may also be revealed in our body."
- 2 Corinthians 1:3: "Praise be to the God and Father of our Lord Jesus Christ, the Father of compassion and the God of all comfort, who comforts us in all our troubles, so that we can comfort those in any trouble with the comfort we ourselves have received from God."
- Philippians 4:13: "I can do everything through him who gives me strength."

As a starting point, these Scriptures teach us that there is more to life than just today. Jackie Kennedy learned this difficult lesson after President Kennedy was assassinated. Just after his death, she wrote to a friend: "There is one thing you must know. I consider that my life is over, and I will spend the rest of it waiting for it really to be over." And she thought it was, when she considered only the immediate moment. But she discovered there is more than the immediate moment, and her life was not over. Instead, she lived a rich and effective life for another thirty years.[2] The psalmist gives us this word of hope in Psalm 30:5, and Paul gives us this word of promise in Romans 8:18. There is more to life than just today.

Also, these Scriptures teach us that there is more to life than our own resources. Corrie Ten Boom provided a helpful illustration of this truth. As a little girl, she told her father one day, "Daddy, I am afraid that I will never be strong enough to be a martyr for Jesus." And her father explained, "Today you do not need the power and the strength to suffer for Jesus, but the moment he gives you the honor of suffering for him, he will also give you all the strength."[3] For Corrie Ten Boom as she faced suffering, for us facing our daily challenges, and for those going through depression, here is a message of hope: we do not have to rely on our own strength. God will also give us his strength. Isaiah 43:2-3, Matthew 11:28, Philippians 4:13, and dozens of other passages herald that promise. There is more to life than our own resources.

Additionally, these Scriptures teach us that there is more to life than our own problems. Paul's word to the Corinthian Christians reminded them—and us—that many people experience difficulties in life. Many people have troubles. Many people are depressed. God's comfort brings relief to us in our suffering. Then, as we receive the comfort of God, we are to be comforters of others. And, in fact, reaching out to comfort others will in itself bring comfort to us (2 Cor 1:3). Focusing on our own problems will lead to the depressing conclusion that our life is in a mess. Focusing on the problems of others will provide a broader perspective, leading eventually to the realization that there is more to life than our own problems.

The Scripture teaches us not only through the specific verses that speak to the issue of depression but also through a remarkable man who modeled the proper response to the disappointments of life that often lead to depression. His name was Job. He provides an excellent model of a person who fleshed out a strategy for overcoming depression.

Job's depression rings forth from the book in the Old Testament known by his name. Note the following verses. Job 3:1 says, "After this, Job opened his mouth and cursed the day of his birth." In Job 3:11, Job asks, "Why did I not perish at birth, and die as I came from the womb?" In Job 3:24, he moans, "For sighing comes to me instead of food; my groans pour out like water." He adds in verse 25: "What I feared has come upon me; what I dreaded has happened to me." And then, he adds further in verse 26: "I have no peace, no quietness; I have no rest, but only turmoil." That sounds like a serious case of depression in the making.

Job's depression arose out of the harsh realities of his life. His oxen were stolen by raiding Sabeans. Fire fell from heaven and destroyed his sheep and the servants who watched them. The Chaldeans stole his camels. A wind blew down the house where his children were and they were all killed. His body was covered with boils. His wife said, "Job, are you still holding on? Why don't you just curse God and die!" Job had good reasons to be depressed.

But Job did not succumb to his problems. Instead, he moved through them and ultimately won victory over them. The first step was to hold his ground when his friends came to offer their explanations. Instead of buying into their explanations of his problem, he took a close look at himself. Then he took his case to God. He confronted God because he believed God was the one from whom the ultimate answer could come. God did not actually answer Job's questions. That is, God didn't give Job an explanation for all of his problems. And yet God did remove Job's depression by reminding Job of God's sovereignty and control of the world. Job did not deny his depression. Nor did he ultimately cave in to his depression. Rather, he took his depression to God and eventually found relief. That relief is articulated in the opening verses of Job 42. Job says to God, "I know that you can do all things; no plan of yours can be thwarted" (v. 2). And then he adds, "Surely I spoke of things I did not understand, things too wonderful for me to know" (v. 3). He adds further, "My ears had heard of you but now my eyes have seen you" (v. 5). Finally he adds, "Therefore I despise myself and repent in dust and ashes" (v. 6). Job ultimately modeled the positive response to the negative emotion called depression.

Set the Strategy

For us to move around this roadblock called depression, simply memorizing a list of Scriptures and marveling at the heroic actions of Job is not enough. Strategies have to be put into place that will enable us translate these principles from Scripture into specific actions in our lives. Let me suggest five strategies.

Strategy #1 is to *check our physical condition*. The first signal that arises out of a continuous problem with depression is a physical one. So the first strategy is to determine if a biological problem is either the primary or the secondary cause of our depression. A visit to the doctor is one of the initial steps for anyone with chronic depression. Sometimes through medication and at other times through dietary recommendations, a doctor can provide assistance in dealing with depression.

We can assist in this process by giving more careful attention to the physical bodies in which we live out our lives. Dr. Richard A Swenson, in his book titled *Margin: Restoring Emotional, Physical, Financial, and Time Reserves to Overloaded Lives,* identifies four gears in the healthiest lifestyle: park, low, drive, and overdrive. Each gear is important: park, the gear in which we renew our spirits and dream; low, the gear for relationships and family; drive, the usual gear for work and play; and overdrive, the gear reserved for the times that require extra effort. "Unfortunately," Dr. Swenson concludes, "many in our society do not shift down from overdrive." He then explains, "Our cars are not meant to race at high speeds continuously—the engine would burn up. Neither are our bodies or spirits."[4] Healthy living, coupled with regular medical consultation, is the first strategy for dealing with one of the root causes of depression.

Strategy #2 is to *check our spiritual condition*. Sometimes depression arises not from a biological disorder but from a spiritual disorder. Guilt can be the seedbed of depression. David clearly experienced this kind of depression in the aftermath of his double sin of adultery with Bathsheba and the subsequent murder of Uriah. In Psalm 32:3-4, David writes, "When I kept silent, my bones wasted away through my groaning all day long. For day and night your hand was heavy upon me; my strength was sapped as in the heat of summer." Relief for David came through confession and repentance, for he adds in Psalm 32:5, "Then I acknowledged my sin to you and did not cover up my iniquity. I said, 'I will confess my transgressions to the LORD'— and you forgave the guilt of my sin." The presence of guilt sapped David's strength and pushed him into depression. Forgiveness removed his guilt and lifted him out of the pit of despair.

Translate David's experience into the spiritual dimension of our relationship with God. A continuing problem with depression might signal a crisis in our spiritual condition. Perhaps guilt has taken root in our lives and has created this spirit of depression. In this case, the strategy is to release that guilt through repentance and confession.

Strategy #3 is to *clarify our standards*. Some Christians are depressed, not because there is something wrong with us physically or spiritually, but because our ambitions and goals are wrong. Failure to reach unrealistic goals often creates a backlash of depression in our lives.

Charles Shultz masterfully depicted this reality in one of his stories about Charlie Brown. Charlie Brown went to see his psychiatrist Lucy because he was depressed. "What's the matter?" she asked. "I'm not having a good day," he replied. She returned, "What do you consider to be a good day?" He explained, "A good day is a day when I meet the girl of my dreams, am elected president of the country, win a Nobel Prize, and hit the game-winning homerun."[5] Charlie Brown's problem was neither biological nor spiritual. Instead, unrealistic goals had pulled Charlie down. He had set impossible standards for himself, and when he did not reach these unrealistic standards, he felt like a failure. His failure, in turn, created a spirit of depression.

When plagued by a continuing experience of depression, examining our goals in light of our gifts and in the context of our circumstances will help us replace unrealistic goals with goals that are more in line with our giftedness and with God's discerned will. We need to clarify our standards.

Strategy #4 is to *build strong relationships*. Most of the causes of depression listed at the beginning of this chapter can be addressed by friends. We find a beautiful expression of this truth in Ecclesiastes 4:9-12:

> Two are better than one, because they have a good return for their work. If one falls down, his friend can help him up. But pity the man who falls and has no one to help him up! Also, if two lie down together, they will keep warm. But how can one keep warm alone? Though one may be overpowered, two can defend themselves. A cord of three strands is not quickly broken.

When in the depths of depression, nothing is more important than to have a friend.

A historic anecdote from the Revolutionary War period underscores the importance of having a friend. Benedict Arnold went from Revolutionary War hero to national villain by his betrayal of the American forces. He escaped to England and spent the remainder of his days without a country, moving from London to Canada and then back to London where he died in 1801. On his deathbed, someone asked if he needed anything. "Yes," he gasped, "a friend."[6] In the depth of his depression, Benedict Arnold was convinced that a friend could somehow help him bear the burden. For us, likewise, establishing and nourishing relationships with others is an effective strategy for battling depression, for two are indeed better than one.

Strategy #5 is to *seek help from a professional counselor.* After we explore all of the strategies cited above, depression might continue to plague our lives. Sometimes we cannot work through our depression on our own. Therefore, another viable strategy for the Christian in the throes of depression is to seek professional help from a counselor. The place to start is with your pastor. Either by providing the counseling you need or by referring you to someone they know, pastors can get you started in finding professional help. Seeking professional help for your depression is not a sign of weakness, nor is it an admission of a lack of faith. It is simply another strategy for helping you move around a roadblock that keeps you from enjoying the abundant life Jesus wants you to experience.

Final Word

Perhaps more so than any of the other roadblocks we have considered, depression is a complex phenomenon with multiple causes and diverse manifestations. Simple solutions will not do. I recognize that. However, rather than wallowing in the mire of our depression with no sense of hope, implementing these strategies is at least a place to start in steering around this major roadblock in the daily pilgrimage of life.

Prayer

Dear God and Father of Light
Break through
The darkness of our depression.

Help us to see
Beyond today and

Beyond our own resources and
Beyond our own problems.

Remind us that
We each reside
In the hollow of
Your strong hands.
And that your grip
Will never slip.

Amen.

NOTES

¹ Nathan S. Kline, *From Sad to Glad* (New York: G. P. Putnam's Sons, 1974), 9, 220.

² Harold I. Smith, *A Decembered Grief* (Kansas City: Beacon Hill Press, 1999), 65.

³ Robert Schuller, *The Be(Happy) Attitudes* (Waco: Word Books, 1985), 218.

⁴ Richard A. Swenson, *Margin* (Colorado Springs CO: Navpress, 1992), 227-28.

⁵ Cecil Osborne, *The Art of Becoming a Whole Person* (Waco: Word Books, 1978), 150.

⁶ Harold I. Smith, *Grieving the Death of a Friend* (Minneapolis: Augsburg, 1996), 22.

When Others Get What We Want

The Envy Roadblock

An ancient tale describes a saintly old hermit who lived in the desert. He was so holy that the evil spirits who tried to lead him into sin were continually defeated and discouraged. They tried everything to break him. They tried temptations of the flesh. They tried to plant doubts in his mind. They even tried to trap him in the sin of pride. Nothing worked. Finally, Satan said to the evil spirits, "You are failing because you are using the wrong method. Let me show you how to do it." Satan went to the holy hermit and whispered in his ear, "Have you heard the good news? Your brother has been appointed Bishop of Alexandria." Immediately, the countenance of the holy hermit changed as he whispered through clinched teeth, "My brother, Bishop of Alexandria!" Envy had taken root in his life.

Envy is one of the most common and most destructive emotions in the human psyche. Envy and jealousy are kin, but envy is the meaner older brother. Jealousy is the desire to have what others have. Envy goes further. Envy not only wants what others have but is also determined to deprive others of what they have. Envy is another roadblock that will keep us from enjoying the full and abundant life Jesus wants us to experience, so it is essential that we discover how to navigate around this roadblock.

Search the Scripture

For the Christian, the place to begin seeking answers is in the word of God. A number of Scriptures address this roadblock called envy.

- Job 5:2: "Resentment kills a fool, and envy slays the simple."
- Psalm 118:24: "This is the day the LORD has made; let us rejoice and be glad in it."
- Proverbs 14:30: "A heart at peace gives life to the body, but envy rots the bones."
- Proverbs 27:4: "Wrath is cruel, and anger is outrageous; but who is able to stand before envy?" (KJV).
- Ecclesiastes 4:4: "And I saw that all labor and all achievement spring from man's envy of his neighbor. This too is meaningless, a chasing after the wind."
- James 3:16: "For where you have envy and selfish ambition, there you find disorder and every evil practice."
- 1 Corinthians 13:4: "Love is patient, love is kind. It does not envy."
- Philippians 4:11: "I am not saying this because I am in need, for I have learned to be content whatever the circumstances."
- 1 Peter 2:1: "Therefore, rid yourselves of all malice and all deceit, hypocrisy, envy, and slander of every kind."

First of all, these Scriptures teach us that life is a gift. We should face each day with gratitude and not envy because each day is a gift from God, something we neither earned nor deserve. Each day is a gift. The proper response to a gift is always gratitude (Ps 118:24) and contentment (Phil 4:11). John Claypool illustrated this essential truth in his response to the tragic death of his daughter. When John Claypool lost his daughter Laura Lue to cancer, he worked through his grief in a series of sermons that formed the nucleus of a best-selling book titled *Tracks of a Fellow Struggler*. In one of these sermons, he told a story from his childhood. When World War II started, a friend of his parents was drafted and the wife decided to stay with her parents while her husband was gone. The wife needed someplace to store her furniture, so the Claypools agreed to keep it. The young family offered the Claypools the use of their washing machine during this time because the Claypools didn't have one. Since John helped with the washing, he became attached to the old washing machine. But eventually, when the war ended, the family returned and reclaimed their furniture, including the washing machine. Young John was quite upset. He did not think it was fair that they had to give up their washing machine. His mother explained, "Son, you must remember that the machine never belonged to us in the first place. That we ever got to use it at all was a gift. So, instead of being mad at its being taken away, let's use this occasion to be grateful that we had it at all."[1] Life is like that for all of us. It is a gift. And the proper attitude toward a gift is always gratitude, not envy.

Secondly, these Scriptures teach us that envy is a destructive force. Envy is more than just a roadblock that blocks our pathway; envy is also a negative force that wreaks destruction in our lives (Prov 14:30) and in the lives of those around us (Jas 3:16). Gary Collins illustrated the destructiveness of envy in an ancient legend of a young Greek athlete who competed at the public games but lost. The public acclaim for the winner, which led to a statue in his honor, kindled a fire of envy in the losing athlete. The loser plotted revenge to destroy the statue created for his adversary. Every night under the cover of darkness the envious young man chiseled at the base of the statue in an attempt to weaken its foundation. Finally, he succeeded. The statue toppled over, but it fell on the disgruntled athlete, who died of "grudgitus." He was not the first, nor will he be the last, to become a victim of his own envy.[2]

In addition, these Scriptures teach us that love and envy are incompatible. Paul puts it this way in the verse from 1 Corinthians 13: "Love does not envy." Love wants the best for others; envy wants the worst for others. They are incompatible desires. Some go through life driven by envy—destroying themselves and everyone with whom they make contact. Others go through life driven by love—developing themselves and everyone with whom they make contact. We must choose, for these are incompatible approaches to life.

These Scriptures can be resources to help us steer around the roadblock of envy. Scripture also teaches us through the stories of individuals who fleshed out these principles in their lives. Consider as a model the man named John who prepared the way for the ministry of Jesus. We know him as John the Baptist. More accurately, he was John the Baptizer, for baptism characterized his ministry. He began his ministry six months before Jesus did and prepared the way for him. In carrying out his assignment, John proved to be a remarkable individual.

To begin with, John was a unique man. He shunned nice clothes for a rough coat made of camel hair. Instead of dining sumptuously, he found his nourishment from a menu of locusts and honey. He was a memorable person, a prophet, unique. He broke the pattern of normal behavior in his day.

John was also a courageous man. Instead of kowtowing to the religious leaders who came out to investigate him, John called them a brood of vipers and challenged them: "Who warned you to flee from the coming wrath?" (Luke 3:7). Instead of approving of the incestuous relationship between Herod and Herod's brother's wife, John reminded Herod he was breaking the law of God (Luke 3:19-20). John was a courageous man. He was one who "tells it like it is."

Further, John was a famous man. When John preached in the wilderness, the Bible says, "The whole Judean countryside and all the people of Jerusalem went out to him" (Mark 1:4). John was the toast of the town. He was the most popular preacher on the circuit. He was a celebrity. That is, he was a celebrity until Jesus came along. After Jesus began preaching, John's popularity fell off. The contrast between John's falling popularity and Jesus' rising popularity came to a head in John 3. Some of John's disciples told him, "Rabbi, that man who was with you on the other side of the Jordan—the one you testified about—well, he is baptizing, and everyone is going to him" (John 3:26). Jesus was now enjoying the popularity John had enjoyed. The crowds who had come to hear John preach now came to hear Jesus. If anyone ever had an excuse to submit to envy, John did.

John responded in a remarkable way. He said, "A man can receive only what is given him from heaven" (John 3:27). And then in verse 30, speaking of Jesus, John adds, "He must become greater; I must become less." We see no envy in John and no resentment about being replaced by Jesus in the favor of the people. Instead, John recognized his place before God and his relationship to Jesus. He did not shun his own opportunities. Instead, he put them in proper perspective. What an example for us to emulate today when others get what we want and what we think we deserve. John the Baptist is a model of how to move around the roadblock of envy.

Set the Strategy

However, we need more than some Scripture references and a sterling example. Getting around this roadblock will require specific strategies. Let me suggest several:

Strategy #1 is to *contemplate the goodness of God.* Envy is not merely a personal issue. Envy also affects our relationship with God. Stephen Shoemaker has correctly concluded that "Envy is a denial of the goodness of God. It wishes to deny God's goodness to others and refuses to recognize God's goodness to oneself."[3] Therefore, an antidote to envy is an adequate comprehension of the goodness of God. The following steps can help us do that. Write down some of the verses in the Bible that describe the goodness of God and read them every day. Keep a journal of God's ongoing provisions. Make a praise list and read it throughout the day. Participate in celebrative worship. Remember the blessings God has already given you. The place to begin in getting a handle on envy is to contemplate the goodness of God.

Strategy #2 is to *establish separate accounts.* Envy not only affects our relationship with God; it also affects our relationships to others. Gary Collins described a strange phenomenon that almost always accompanies the feeling of envy. Collins said, "Envy is like a cancer which slowly and subtly takes over a person's thinking so that the envious man feels others' fortunes are his misfortunes; their profit, his loss; their blessing, his bane; their health, his illness; their promotion, his demotion; their success, his failure."[4] That is a keen insight into the way envy works. Steven Covey calls this phenomenon the "scarcity mentality." The scarcity mentality pictures life as one big pie. If someone else gets a big piece of the pie, that leaves only a small piece of the pie for us. This scarcity mentality feeds our envy, for it convinces us that if someone else receives special recognition or remarkable success, then something is taken away from us.[5]

Therefore an antidote to envy is to develop the abundance mentality that life has enough abundance for everyone. This is what I mean by "establishing separate accounts." God's dealing with others does not in any way detract from the way God deals with us. What God provides for others does not in any way diminish what God can provide for us. Like parents whose complete love goes out to every child, no matter how many children they have, God is a loving Father whose graciousness is not diminished by the increasing number of his children. One of the strategies for defusing our envy is to recognize that God deals with each of us through separate accounts.

Strategy #3 is to *avoid comparisons*. Envy affects our relationships with others in another way. When driven by the scarcity mentality, it is easy for us to measure our blessings by the blessings of others. Comparing our lives with the lives of others, observing them from our limited perspective, often leads us to match our paucity with their plenty. Such comparisons feed our envy. Consequently, our envy says, "I wish I could exchange my life for the life of that other person." This is one of the primary causes of envy, and it can strike anyone. Our marriage is not as good as their marriage. Our house is not as big as their house. Our church is not as large as their church. Such comparisons always feed our envy. But a fatal flaw mars the comparison of our lives to the lives of others. We do not always know what that other person's life is really like. American poet Edwin Arlington Robinson wrote a dramatic poem titled "Richard Cory" that captures this truth.

Whenever Richard Cory went down town,
We people on the pavement looked at him;
He was a gentleman from sole to crown,
Clean favored, and imperially slim.

And he was always quietly arrayed,
And he was always human when he talked;
But still he fluttered pulses when he said,
"Good morning," and he glittered when he walked.

And he was rich—yes, richer than a king—
And admirably schooled in every grace;
In fine, we thought that he was everything
To make us wish that we were in his place.

So on we worked, and waited for the light,
And went without the meat, and cursed the bread;
And Richard Cory, one calm summer night,
Went home and put a bullet through his head.[6]

The old Indian proverb warns us not to judge another person until we have walked a mile in his moccasins. I am suggesting that we not *envy* another person until we have walked a mile in his moccasins, for we do not know from the outside everything that person is going through on the inside. An antidote for envy therefore is to remember that every person has both blessings and burdens and that the most productive person is the one who learns to appreciate his own blessings and live with his own burdens.

Final Word

Shakespeare was right. Envy is "the green-eyed monster which doth mock the meat it feeds on"—and what it feeds on is the envious person's soul. It is another roadblock that will prevent us from experiencing the full and abundant life Jesus wants us to enjoy. To get around the roadblock of envy, here are three specific strategies: contemplate the goodness of God, establish separate accounts, and avoid comparisons.

Prayer

Dear Lord
The one from whom
Every good and perfect gift comes
Forgive us when
Our greed overcomes our gratitude
And when our desire
For what others have
Blinds us to the blessings
Of what we already have.

Help us to desire the giver
More than the gifts.

And instead of always wanting more
Help us simply to appreciate more
What we already have.

Amen.

NOTES

[1] John Claypool, *Tracks of a Fellow Struggler* (Waco: Word Books, 1974), 76.

[2] Gary Collins, *Overcoming Anxiety* (Santa Ana CA: Vision House Publishers, 1973), 106.

[3] H. Stephen Shoemaker, *The Jekyll & Hyde Syndrome* (Nashville: Broadman Press, 1987), 55.

[4] Collins, *Overcoming Anxiety*, 108.

[5] Stephen R. Covey, *The Seven Habits of Highly Effective People* (New York: Simon and Schuster, 1989), 219.

[6] Anthony Campolo, *Seven Deadly Sins* (Wheaton IL: Victor Books, 1989), 105.

When We Blow It

The Failure Roadblock

It was fall 1973. The scene was Waco, Texas. The setting was Baylor Stadium. On homecoming weekend, alumni returned from all over the country to watch the Bears play football. The opponent was Texas Christian University. Those of us there that day will never forget what we saw. Baylor played dismally from the opening kickoff. With eleven minutes left in the game, TCU led by 34-7. Suddenly, Baylor began a comeback, led by quarterback Neal Jeffrey. Three quick touchdowns brought the score to 34-28, with two minutes left. Baylor stopped TCU again, received the punt, and moved toward the goal line for what would be the winning touchdown. Baylor was on the 6-yard line. The first and second down plays moved the ball back to the 11-yard line. Baylor called their last timeout and Neal Jeffrey went to the sideline to get the play. He returned to the field to face third down and 11 yards to go for the touchdown, with 43 seconds in the game. Jeffrey threw a pass, but the receiver was tackled for a loss. The ball was on the 14-yard line. What would Jeffrey do? He rushed the team quickly to the line of scrimmage, took the snap, and threw the ball out of bounds to stop the clock. What Neal Jeffrey forgot was that it was fourth down. The ball went over to TCU; the game was lost.

Each of us has been in that spot at one time or another. Fourth down, no timeouts, time running out, victory within our grasp, and everyone depending on us—and then we blew it. Each of us knows what it means to fail at something. Unfortunately, this failure often becomes a roadblock that keeps us from experiencing the abundant life Jesus wants for us. All of us need a strategy for moving around this roadblock. The place to begin, for the Christian, is the Scripture.

Search the Scripture

The Bible gives helpful advice on how to navigate around this particular roadblock. Here are a few verses to consider.

- Psalm 37:24: "Though he stumble, he will not fall, for the LORD upholds him with his hand."
- Jonah 3:1: "Then the word of the LORD came to Jonah a second time."
- John 8:10-11: "He straightened up and asked her, 'Woman, where are they? Has no one condemned you?' 'No one, sir,' she said. 'Then neither do I condemn you,' Jesus declared. 'Go now and leave your life of sin.'"
- Romans 8:38-39: "For I am convinced that neither death nor life, neither angels nor demons, neither the present nor the future, nor any powers, neither height nor depth, nor anything else in all creation, will be able to separate us from the love of God that is in Christ Jesus our Lord."
- Galatians 6:1: "Brothers, if someone is caught in a sin, you who are spiritual should restore him gently."
- 1 John 1:9: "If we confess our sins, he is faithful and just and will forgive us our sins and purify us from all unrighteousness."

These Scriptures reveal that God is a God of the second chance. Jonah is an excellent case in point. God called Jonah to take his word to the Ninevites. Jonah refused to go. He disobeyed God. In fact, he went in the opposite direction from where God sent him. If ever a biblical character failed in an assignment from God, Jonah was that character. Yet God came to Jonah and gave him a chance to make a new beginning (Jonah 3:1). And he'll do the same for us.

Further, these Scriptures reflect the limitations of failure. For example, the psalmist reminds us that God does not allow our failures to be terminal.

He holds our hand and sets us on our feet so that we can continue to serve him (Ps 37:24). Paul, in his epistle to the Romans, reminds us that the heartache, suffering, and difficulties that often confront us in life as a result of our failures will never diminish our value before God nor disrupt our connection with God (Rom 8:38-39). Also, John in his epistle reminds us that confession brings forgiveness for any sin committed (1 John 1:9). No failure is final with God. That is the consistent proclamation of Scripture.

These Scriptures then illustrate the proper response to the failure of others. Since God gives us a second chance after our failures, we must be willing to give a second chance to those around us who fail. Even when others are caught in their failure, even when their failure becomes public knowledge, the proper response on our part is not condemnation but restoration (Gal 6:1). Instead, as God gives to us the grace to make a new beginning, that grace should be extended to others.

Write down these Scriptures. Memorize them. Inculcate their truths into your life. They will provide motivation when failure blocks your way. The search for a biblical character who models /these promises of Scripture focuses the spotlight on John Mark. He provides an unforgettable example in the Bible of one who experienced failure and then overcame it.

Apparently, John Mark lived in Jerusalem. Tradition affirms that he was the son of Mary, a woman who played a significant part in the life of the early church. For example, some scholars believe the Upper Room in which Jesus observed his last meal with his disciples was in her home. Luke tells us in his story of the early church that she had a house in which Christians met for prayer (Acts 12:1-16). Consequently, John Mark was probably an eyewitness to some of the most important early events of the church. It is no surprise, then, that when Paul and Barnabas set out on their first missionary journey, they decided to take John Mark with them as their assistant. The surprise is what happened along the way. The key verse is Acts 13:13. Here was a young man of promise, a young man who had every opportunity to contribute mightily to God's kingdom work. Yet, Acts 13:13 reveals that he came to a point where he said, "God, I'm through. I'm not going to go any further. I quit." John Mark had a chance to make history, but he blew it. He is a biblical poster child for failure.

However, Acts 13:13 is not the final chapter in John Mark's life. It is only the first chapter. Following this first chapter of failure is the story of John Mark's comeback. John Mark appears again on the radar screen in Acts 15:39. Paul and Barnabas wanted to take a second mission trip to revisit the churches they had founded. When Barnabas insisted John Mark be taken along, Paul resisted. Consequently, Paul and Barnabas split. Paul took Silas, and verse 39 says, "Barnabas took Mark and sailed for Cyprus." Paul had apparently given up on young John Mark, but Barnabas had not. With Barnabas's encouragement, Mark returned to the work of the Lord.

The next piece of the story is Colossians 4:10. Paul was in prison in Rome. The year was about AD 63. Paul wrote a letter to the Christians at the city of Colossae and included this statement at the end: "My fellow prisoner Aristarchus sends you his greetings, as does Mark, the cousin of Barnabas." Here we see Mark and Paul reconciled and Mark again vitally involved in God's work. Mark had not only mended his relationship with God; he had also been restored in his relationship with Paul.

A further reference is found in 2 Timothy 4:11. Paul was in prison in Rome, probably a second imprisonment, about AD 67, shortly before his death. At this point only Luke was with Paul, and he gave this instruction to Timothy: "Get Mark and bring him with you, because he is helpful to me in my ministry." Paul's attitude toward Mark morphed from rejection to acceptance to celebration. What a change from Acts 15 when Paul would not even allow Mark to be with him.

Perhaps the most important piece in this final chapter of John Mark's amazing comeback is the Gospel of Mark. Of the four accounts of Jesus' life included in our New Testament, one of them—the earliest, the clearest, and the most concise—was written by this man who at one point in his life had quit on God, gone home, and apparently had been lost to God's cause. The first picture of Mark shows him to be a failure; the final picture of Mark shows him once more serving God. Mark moved past failure to effectiveness. He is a model of how to move around the roadblock called failure.

Set the Strategy

The example of Mark and the Scriptures cited above provided the resources to construct strategies for moving past our failures today. Let me suggest three.

Strategy #1 is to *think the right thoughts*. Chuck Swindoll has pointed out that nothing is more important in life than our attitude. He writes, "I believe the single most significant decision I can make on a day-to-day basis is my choice of attitude. It is more important than my past, my education, my bankroll, my successes or failures, fame or pain, what other people think of me or say about me, my circumstances, or my position."[1]

If nothing is more important in dealing with failures than our attitude, then the first strategy in dealing with our failure is to approach it with the right attitude. Two choices face us: universalizing our failure or individualizing it. Let me illustrate the difference. To universalize our failure is to say about our failure, "I always mess up. That is just like me. And what's more, next time I'll probably fail again." Universalizing our failure leads us to expand a single failure experience into the universal description of our lives. On the other hand, to individualize our failure is to say about our failure, "I hardly ever mess up. This is not like me. And what's more, next time I'll get it right." Individualizing our failure enables us to separate a single failure experience from the other experiences of our lives. Thus, the recognition that we often fail does not make us a failure.

Choosing to individualize our failure rather than universalizing prevents us from accepting the "failure" label and prompts us to move around our failure. So this is the first step in dealing with our failure: think the right thoughts about it. Do not universalize the experience—individualize it.

Strategy #2 is to *ask the right questions.* Just individualizing our failure is not enough. We must also be willing to learn from our failure by asking the right questions about it. This was the secret of Thomas Edison's productive life. Edison experienced repeated failures. However, for him, every failure was a stepping-stone to some future success. For example, after thousands of experiments on a certain project had failed to uncover anything, one of Edison's colleagues was decimated. "We've learned nothing," the associate whined. But Edison responded instead with this word of hope: "I cheerily assured him that we had learned something, for we had learned for certainty that the thing couldn't be done that way, and that we would have to try some other way."[2]

This is the second step in dealing with our failure: ask the right questions. When failure comes, don't waste time asking, "Why did this happen?" and seeking some scapegoat to blame for the failure. Instead, ask the question, "What can I learn from this experience?" The answers to this second question will steer us around the temporary roadblock created by our experience of failure.

Strategy #3 is to *do the right things*. Thinking the right thoughts means to individualize the experience of failure instead of universalizing it. Asking the right questions means to learn lessons from the experience of failure. Both steps are important. And yet both steps together are not enough. After individualizing the experience of failure and after taking from it lessons for life, the key is to put those lessons into practice. The right thoughts and right questions must motivate us to do the right things.

Let me illustrate with a simple story. A pilot landed his plane on a rough landing strip on the side of the mountain to pick up two hunters. When he saw they had bagged two elk, he refused to load them on his plane because the animals weighed too much and he was afraid the plane would crash when he tried to elevate over the surrounding mountains. "Last year," one of the hunters protested, "we bagged two elk of the same weight and the pilot didn't object." The pilot finally gave in, loaded the men and their equipment and the dead animals, and took off. However, the weight was too much, just as the pilot had feared, and the plane crashed into the side of the mountain. All three men survived. The pilot asked, "Does anyone know where we are?" "Yes," the hunter said, "We're about 50 yards from where we crashed last year!"

After learning the lessons of our previous experiences of failure, we cannot simply repeat the same mistake, or we'll end up crashing in the same place year after year. Instead, the lessons from the past must motivate us to follow new patterns and to practice new behaviors. This is the third step in dealing with our failure: do the right things. The next time failure comes, determine what led to the failure and then do something different.

Final Word

Failure is a part of every life, but it does not have to be the defining characteristic of our lives. Like John Mark, each of us can move past our failures and once more become effective servants of God. Here are the key strategies: think the right thoughts, ask the right questions, do the right things.

P.S.: By the way, here's the "rest of the story" concerning Neal Jeffrey's failure in that homecoming football game against TCU. That event occurred in fall 1973. The next year, this same Baylor quarterback, who had failed so publicly in the homecoming game of a year before, took Baylor to the promised land, for 1974 was the year when Baylor won the Southwest Conference Championship for the first time in fifty years. Neal moved from Baylor failure to Baylor legend. Simply another reminder that no failure need be final!

Prayer

Dear God
Of new beginnings
Help us to begin again
With you today.

We recognize our failure,
We regret our failure,
And now
We release our failure.

Help us now
To focus on you
Instead of ourselves
To focus on the future
Instead of the past
To focus on
What we can be
Instead of
What we are.

Amen.

NOTES

[1] Charles R. Swindoll, *Strengthening Your Grip* (Waco: Word Books, 1982), 207.

[2] Ronald W. Clark, *Edison: The Man Who Made the Future* (New York: G. P. Putnam's Sons, 1977), 71.

Roadblock #11

When We Feel Too Bad to Feel Good

The Guilt Roadblock

In T. S. Eliot's work *The Cocktail Party*, the author describes a woman named Celia who is talking to her psychiatrist, Reilly. She is burdened by something she has done. Reilly asks her what her parents taught her about sin. She explains that they discarded the word. She goes on to say that they considered ignorant and unlearned anyone who seemed to be overly concerned with guilt. After a brief pause, she continued, "But I have not been able to dispose of the feeling of personal failure so easily. I continue to be bothered by a feeling of uncleanness, a feeling of emptiness, of failure toward someone or something outside myself. And I feel I must . . . atone, is that the word?"[1]

Discard the words "sin" and "guilt" and "atone" if you want to. Yet, like this woman in T. S. Eliot's story, the feelings of uncleanness or emptiness or failure still raise their menacing heads. Even describing our problem as a phobia or a complex or a neurosis does not bring relief. Whatever the attempt to camouflage it, the reality of guilt is nevertheless present in our lives, and it often becomes a roadblock that prevents us from experiencing the full and abundant life God wants for us. We must develop a strategy for moving around this roadblock.

Search the Scripture

For the Christian, the place to begin in seeking answers is the Scripture. Several Scriptures provide insights for dealing with our guilt.

- Psalm 38:4: "My guilt has overwhelmed me like a burden too heavy to bear."
- Psalm 103:12: "As far as the east is from the west, so far has he removed our transgressions from us."
- Isaiah 1:18: "Though your sins are like scarlet, they shall be as white as snow."
- Isaiah 6:5: "'Woe to me!' I cried. 'I am ruined! For I am a man of unclean lips, and I live among a people of unclean lips, and my eyes have seen the King, the Lord Almighty.'"
- Jeremiah 33:8: "I will cleanse them from all the sin they have committed against me and will forgive all their sins of rebellion against me."
- Malachi 3:7: "'Return to me, and I will return to you,' says the LORD Almighty."
- Matthew 4:17: "From that time on Jesus began to preach, 'Repent, for the kingdom of heaven is near.'"
- Luke 5:8: "When Simon Peter saw this, he fell at Jesus' knees and said, 'Go away from me, Lord; I am a sinful man!'"
- 1 John 1:9: "If we confess our sins, he is faithful and just and will forgive us our sins and purify us from all unrighteousness."

These Scriptures underscore the reality of guilt. Paul Tillich, a famous American theologian of the past, once said that it is impossible to have a sensitive conscience and a good conscience at the same time.[2] Anyone with a modicum of self-awareness recognizes his guilt. From Adam to David to Isaiah to Simon Peter (Gen 3; Ps 38:4; Isa 6:5; Luke 5:8) to every person reading this chapter, guilt is a universal experience of humankind. Imagine this courtroom scene. The trial is already under way. The accused stands up and says, "Your honor, I'd like to change my plea. I wish to plead guilty." The judge is taken aback. "I don't understand," he replied, "You said you were innocent at the beginning of the trial. Why are you changing your plea?" The accused explained, "Well, I thought I was innocent, but at that time, I hadn't heard all the evidence against me!" Once we are confronted with all of the evidence against us, each of us must plead guilty. Our heart confirms the clear message of Scripture: guilt is a universal experience of humankind.

In addition, these Scriptures point toward a remedy for guilt. They provide the reminder that our guilt can be released through God's forgiveness (Ps 34; Mal 3:7; 1 John 1:9). Again, use your imagination. A middle-aged Christian is sitting in her pastor's office discussing the Christian life. The pastor describes his daily devotional experience with God in which he says he actually talks with God and God talks with him. The woman is somewhat skeptical about her pastor's claims, so she decides to test him. "If you directly speak to God and if God directly speaks to you, then let me ask you to do something for me. The next time you talk to him, ask him what terrible sin I committed when I was in college." The activity to which the woman referred was something no one ever knew about except her and God. The guilt of this sin had burdened her for years. She wanted relief from her guilt but didn't know how to find it. The pastor agreed to ask God about her sin. Several weeks later, the woman bumped into her pastor in the hallway on a Sunday morning. "Well," she asked, "did you and God have one of your talks?" "Yes," the pastor responded, "we did." The woman continued, "And did you ask him what sin I committed in college?" The pastor replied, "Yes, I did." Pushing the pastor further, the woman queried, "And what did God say?" The pastor responded, "He said, 'I don't remember.'"

Like that Christian woman, many of us carry around a load of guilt about something God has long ago forgotten. The Christian does not have to carry around this feeling of guilt. The Christian does not have to be burdened by the wrongs committed. The remedy is to put our guilt into the hands of a loving God.

Finally, these Scriptures describe the results of that remedy for guilt (Ps 103:12; Jer 33:8). One of the clearest biblical images of that result comes in the word "forgiveness" (1 John 1:9). The Greek word translated "forgiveness" means "to send away" and pictures someone taking our guilt and sending it away, thus removing it from our view. For example, the prophet Isaiah pictures forgiveness as something that cleanses us and makes us white as snow (Isa 1:18). And, in Jesus' story of the Prodigal Son, forgiveness is pictured as reconciliation with those from whom we have been estranged (Luke 15). Release, cleansing, and reconciliation—these are just a few of the New Testament images to describe the result that comes through forgiveness.

These Scriptures provide a beginning point for moving around the road-block of guilt. Further lessons come from a biblical character who knew both the depth of guilt and the releasing power of forgiveness. His name was David. Most of us are familiar with the general sketch of David's experience with Bathsheba (2 Sam 11–12). Instead of going out to battle with his troops, King David stayed at home. From his elevated position on the roof of his palace, David's eyes could sweep across the city of Jerusalem. As he looked around, his eyes fell on a beautiful young woman who was bathing. Her name was Bathsheba. David was captured by her beauty and desired to be with her, so he sent for her, slept with her, and then sent her back home. That was not, however, the end of the story. Bathsheba revealed to David that she was pregnant. The fact that her husband was out in the field insured that everyone would know someone other than her husband was the father of this child. David should have come clean at that point. However, instead of admitting his sin, David tried to cover it up. He brought Bathsheba's husband Uriah home and provided an opportunity for him to be with his wife. Uriah refused, explaining that he would not go in to be with his wife while his fellow soldiers were out in the field. David's coverup attempt fell through. That was still not the end of the story. Instead of admitting his sin at this point, David devised a plan by which Uriah would be killed in battle. Then he could take Bathsheba into his harem and no one would ever know what he had done.

Even that was not the end of the story. God sent the prophet Nathan to confront David with his sin. Confronted by Nathan the prophet, David finally did what he should have done in the beginning. He acknowledged his sin, confessed it before God, and experienced God's forgiveness. The steps to his recovery are spelled out in Psalm 32. Listen to his poignant agony: "When I kept silent, my bones wasted away through my groaning all day long. For day and night your hand was heavy upon me; my strength was sapped as in the heat of summer. Then I acknowledged my sin to you and did not cover up my iniquity. I said, 'I will confess my transgressions to the LORD'—and you forgave the guilt of my sin" (Ps 32:2-5). After a few inappropriate attempts to deal with his guilt, David finally took the pathway that led to forgiveness and renewal. He is a model to help us move around the roadblock of guilt in our lives.

Set the Strategy

Like David—though perhaps not in the same way—each of us has sinned. And the inevitable result of our sin is guilt. David's example and the Scriptures cited above can provide resources for establishing a strategy to move around the roadblock of guilt in our lives. Let me quickly catalogue some strategies.

Strategy #1 is to *avoid inappropriate strategies.* One inappropriate strategy is evasion—denying the reality of our guilt or refusing to accept responsibility for it. Our attempt at evading the responsibility for our guilt will be no more successful than David's attempt at evasion reflected in Psalms 32 and 51.

Another inappropriate strategy is projection—blaming our problem on someone else and attempting to cleanse ourselves of guilt by condemning or destroying the other person. This is a common psychological ploy. Unfortunately, it is no more effective as a means of escaping our guilt than is the pathway of evasion.

Yet another inappropriate strategy is relativization—reducing the seriousness of what we have done by pointing out how many others do the same. Barbara Brown Taylor is right on target when she writes, "Abandoning the language of sin will not make sin go away. Human beings will continue to experience alienation, deformation, damnation, and death no matter what we call them. Abandoning the language will simply leave us speechless before them, and increase our denial of their presence in our lives."[3] These strategies do not lead to recovery but to continued problems and therefore are not effective strategies for moving around this roadblock.

Strategy #2 is to *clarify the source and nature of our guilt.* We should begin by distinguishing between legitimate and illegitimate guilt. Illegitimate guilt is feeling guilty about something caused by someone else, feeling guilty about something beyond our power to change, or feeling guilty about something done out of ignorance. Illegitimate guilt, in other words, is guilt that is not congruent with the situation.

Real guilt weighs too much for us to load up our lives further with illegitimate guilt evolving from unreasonable demands from others and unrealistic expectations from ourselves. The place to begin in moving past our guilt is to analyze it. What is the cause of our guilt? Was our action the source of this guilt? Could the situation have been handled in a more effective way? Did we know what we were doing? Clarifying the source and nature of the problem will enable us to distinguish between legitimate guilt and illegitimate guilt.

Strategy #3 is to *confess to God.* If, after clarifying the source and nature of the problem, it becomes clear that the guilt is legitimate, then we must release our guilt to the only one who can help us, and that is God. Only God can forgive us; only God can take the burden of our guilt away; and only God can liberate us to make a new beginning.

Guilt is released through confession. Confession is more than just saying, "I'm sorry for what I have done." The word "confess" literally means to agree with or to say the same thing as another. To confess our sins to God, therefore, means to say the same thing about our sin as God would say. To confess is to agree with God about our sin. Our confession needs to be specific as we name our sins. And it needs to be immediate, for holding on to our sin delays the release that comes from God's forgiveness.

Since God promises to forgive our sins once they are confessed (1 John 1:9), we can confidently confess our sins to God knowing that God will forgive our sin. The confidence of God's forgiveness should then free us to forgive ourselves.

Strategy #4 is to *change our actions.* To avoid getting into a sin-confession-forgiveness-sin cycle, the fourth strategy is deliberately to change our actions, our attitudes, and our aspirations that have produced the guilt. Let me give one example of this. In a small country church each year at revival time, one of the older members would pray, "Oh, Lord, please wipe the cobwebs of guilt out of my life." Next year, at revival time, he would stand up and pray the same prayer. "Oh, Lord, please wipe the cobwebs of guilt out of my life." Finally, when he again stood up and voiced that prayer, one of the youngsters who had heard the same prayer year after year stood up and said, "No, God—kill the spider!" Instead of praying that God will wipe the cobwebs of guilt out of our lives, each of us needs to kill the spider. That means changing the actions and attitudes and aspirations that have produced the guilt.

Final Word

Not one of us will avoid the experience of sin or the feeling of guilt that always accompanies it. As Carlyle Marney once put it, "It is too late for us to worry about innocence. Our only choice now is how to be responsible in our guilt."[4] Implementing the following strategies will enable us to be responsible in our guilt: avoidance, clarification, confession, and change. And being responsible in our guilt is one of the ways to move toward the full and abundant life God wants us to experience through Jesus Christ.

Prayer

O Holy God
Like David we groan
In your presence
For we are unholy
In our actions and
In our attitudes,
In our words and
In our ways.

Wipe us clean
With your forgiveness
And then empower us
Through your Spirit
To be holy
As you are holy.

Amen.

NOTES

[1] John R. Claypool, *The Light Within You* (Waco: Word, 1983), 184.

[2] Rollo May, *Paulus: Reminiscences of a Friendship* (New York: Harper & Row, 1973), 76.

[3] Barbara Brown Taylor, *Speaking of Sin: The Lost Language of Salvation* (Cambridge: Cowley Publications, 2000), 5.

[4] John R. Claypool, "Render Unto Caesar and Unto God," sermon preached at Broadway Baptist Church in Ft. Worth, 4 July 1976.

When We Can't Get Out of Bed

The Immobilization Roadblock

She was doing everything she could to get him out of bed so he could go to church. She threatened him and begged him. She even poured water on him. Nothing worked. He was adamant: "I am not going to church. The deacons don't like me. The teachers hate to see me coming. The ministers can't stand me. I'm not going." As patiently as she could, she countered his argument with this reminder: "You have to go to church for three reasons. First, it is the right thing to do. Second, it is important to set a good example. And third, you are the pastor of the church. You have to go!"

It is not just pastors who have trouble getting out of bed in the morning. All of us have that difficulty at times. This is in fact one of the basic issues of life for all of us: how to stay motivated to face daily challenges. I'm not talking about how to motivate others. The greatest motivational challenge is the challenge to motivate ourselves. An anonymous poet expressed the dilemma like this:

I spent a fortune on a trampoline
A stationary bike and a rowing machine,
Complete with gadgets to measure my pulse
And others to show my progress results
And gadgets to measure the miles I had charted
But they forgot the gadget
To get me started!

That is an important gadget—the gadget to get us started! Finding that gadget is essential for us to move around this roadblock of immobilization and thus experience the abundant life Jesus wants us to enjoy.

Search the Scripture

For the Christian, the place to begin in seeking answers is the Bible. Many Scriptures address this particular roadblock. Let me list a few of them.

- Ecclesiastes 9:10: "Whatever your hand finds to do, do it with all your might, for in the grave, where you are going, there is neither working nor planning nor knowledge nor wisdom."
- Ecclesiastes 11:6: "Sow your seed in the morning, and at evening let not your hands be idle, for you do not know which will succeed, whether this or that, or whether both will do equally well."
- Jeremiah 31:29-30: "In those days people will no longer say, 'The fathers have eaten sour grapes, and the children's teeth are set on edge.' Instead, everyone will die for his own sin; whoever eats sour grapes—his own teeth will be set on edge."
- Luke 12:48: "From everyone who has been given much, much will be demanded; and from the one who has been entrusted with much, much more will be asked."
- 1 Corinthians 3:12-15: "If any man builds on this foundation using gold, silver, costly stones, wood, hay, or straw, his work will be shown for what it is, because the day will bring it to light. It will be revealed with fire, and the fire will test the quality of each man's work. If what he has built survives, he will receive his reward. If it is burned up, he will suffer loss; he himself will be saved, but only as one escaping through the flames."
- James 4:13: "Now listen, you who say, 'Today or tomorrow we will go to this or that city, spend a year there, carry on business and make money.'

Why, you do not even know what will happen tomorrow. What is your life? You are a mist that appears for a little while and then vanishes."
- 2 Peter 3:11-12: "Since everything will be destroyed in this way, what kind of people ought you to be? You ought to live holy and godly lives as you look forward to the day of God and speed its coming."

First of all, these Scriptures verify that time is short. As a result, every Christian must take advantage of the time given us. It is a dangerous thing to put off until tomorrow the challenges that are before us today. No one knows that tomorrow will come. Ecclesiastes 9:10 and James 4:13-15 clearly sound that warning.

Further, these Scriptures acknowledge that the results of our actions are unpredictable. Because of this, Christians should diversify their efforts to maximize the possible returns. It is perilous to put all of our efforts in a single project that promises large profits. As Ecclesiastes 11:6 clearly affirms, this venture may fail.

These Scriptures also certify that all are responsible to carry their load. As a result, Christians should not expect someone else to do our part for us, nor can we depend on anyone else to carry out our assignment. Each of us must do our own part (Jer 31:29-30; Luke 12:48).

Finally, these Scriptures declare that judgment is certain. As a result, every Christian will someday have to give an account for how we have lived out our lives. We cannot live life as if there were no consequences to our actions. Each of us is accountable to God (1 Cor 3:12-15; 2 Pet 3:11-12).

Those lessons provide a starting place for our strategy to move around the roadblock of immobilization. Further lessons come from the sterling example of one of the most motivated individuals in Christian history—the man named Paul. His emergence as the most significant figure in early Christian history is a remarkable story. In the beginning, Paul actively opposed Christianity, even participating in the murder of a Christian leader named Stephen. Consequently, when he became a Christian, most of the church leaders were suspicious of him. He had to overcome that suspicion before he could become integrated into the life of the first century church. In addition, some portraits from early church history attribute to Paul a less than appealing physical appearance—bowed legs, eyebrows that connected in the middle, a hooked nose! Further, he was plagued throughout his ministry by a terrible burden he referred to as his "thorn in the flesh" (2 Cor 12:7). What's more, he was constantly hounded by a core group of opponents who followed him wherever he went and stirred up the church against him (Acts 17:13). Then, as he continued to serve Christ, he was beaten and stoned on more than one occasion. He was arrested and spent a great deal of time in jail (2 Cor 11:23-27). If ever anyone had an excuse not to get out of bed in the morning, Paul did. The fact that he overcame all of these obstacles to become the leading figure in early Christendom gives evidence of his self-motivation. To discover the secret of Paul's motivation, we need to turn our attention to specific Scriptures.

In 1 Corinthians 9:27, for example, Paul says, "I beat my body and make it my slave so that after I have preached to others, I myself will not be disqualified for the prize." This verse points to fear as a motivation—Paul's fear that he would not be faithful all the way to the end. That fear overcame the threat of immobility.

In 2 Corinthians 5:10, Paul says, "For we must all appear before the judgment seat of Christ, that each one may receive what is due him for the things done while in the body, whether good or bad." This verse points to accountability as a motivation—Paul's recognition that he would have to give an account to God for what he had done with his life. Awareness of that day of accountability before God motivated him.

In 2 Corinthians 5:14, Paul says, "For Christ's love compels us." This verse points to love as a motivation—the love of God for Paul that motivated him to share that love with the world.

In Galatians 2:20, Paul says, "I have been crucified with Christ and I no longer live, but Christ lives in me. The life I live in the body, I live by faith in the Son of God, who loved me and gave himself for me." This verse points to empowerment as a motivator—the power of God that had been set loose in Paul's life through the indwelling Christ. Tapping that power motivated Paul to action.

Finally, in Philippians 3:13-14, Paul says, "Brothers, I do not consider myself yet to have taken hold of it. But one thing I do: Forgetting what is behind and straining toward what is ahead, I press on toward the goal to win the prize for which God has called me heavenward in Christ Jesus." This verse points to focus as a motivator—Paul's willingness to focus his energy on one central goal and not allow anything to keep him from pursuing that goal. That focus energized Paul for action.

Paul was motivated not from the external circumstances of his life but from these inner commitments: fear, accountability, love, empowerment, and focus. Paul provides a model for the kind of self-motivation that will enable us to move around the roadblock of immobilization.

Set the Strategy

The lessons from Paul's life and the lessons from the Scriptures cited above provide a resource pool from which to construct strategies for getting out of bed every morning and thus steering around this roadblock.

Strategy #1 is to *cultivate our inner life.* What an example Mother Teresa provides for instituting this strategy. Mother Teresa spent nearly half a century in the midst of the world's squalor and poverty, helping people live with courage and die with dignity. Someone asked her once what energized her and enabled her to work from before dawn until midnight every day for so many decades. She explained, "I take the blessed sacrament every morning." She was referring to the presence of God in her life, which she found in the sacrament. This presence of God in her life animated and energized and motivated her.[1]

To be motivated to get out of bed every morning requires that same energizing presence of God in our lives. Daily time with God in prayer is essential. Regular time in God's word is required. Meditation on God's plan is mandatory. Cultivating the inner life provides an energy source for carrying out our plans. The first strategy, then, is to develop a daily and weekly discipline that will keep us in close personal touch with God.

Strategy #2 is to *strengthen our connections.* Cultivating our inner life will strengthen our relationship with God. We must also strengthen our relationships with others who are around us. Life is not a solo journey but a joint effort. This network of relationships, both those with God and those with other human beings, will continuously inspire us to action.

One night in 1945, General Dwight Eisenhower walked along the Rhine, thinking of a major initiative that would begin the next morning. He met a soldier and asked him why he wasn't sleeping. The young GI didn't recognize the supreme allied commander. "I guess I'm a little nervous," the GI said. "Well," said Eisenhower, "so am I. Let's walk together by the river and perhaps we'll draw strength from each other."[2] To be motivated to get out of bed every morning, we need other people with whom we are connected and from whom we can draw strength and inspiration and insight. The second strategy, then, is to establish a structure by which to connect our lives with one or more people who will be our mentors and to whom we will be accountable.

Strategy #3 is to *clarify our goals*. Knowing where we are going also motivates us. Goals have a magnetic effect on us, enticing us out of the reality of today toward the promise of tomorrow.

Popular entertainer Dolly Parton acknowledged that she has been drawn forward by her goals. Dolly Parton was born the fourth child of twelve children to a poor family in Sevier County, Tennessee. Neither of her parents was educated, and she grew up in the poverty of the hill country. Yet, today, she has become one of the most well-known and successful entertainers in America. She had to overcome a great deal to reach the level where she is now. In her autobiography, she reveals what motivated her. Recalling her Christian conversion experienced as a child and describing how she felt in that experience, she explains the desire to use music to touch other people's lives: "I knew my dreams of making music, of traveling outside the Smokies and pursuing a greater purpose, were not silly childhood ideas but grand real schemes ordained and cocreated by my newfound heavenly father." As she describes each of the barriers she had to overcome, she explains that "I would have quit had it not been for my dreams."[3]

Dolly Parton was motivated by her dreams, not only to get out of bed each day but to overcome mountains of obstacles to become a superstar. To be motivated to get out of bed every morning requires a similar understanding of what we want to accomplish with our lives. As an oft-used cliché puts it, "We may not make our goals, but our goals will make us." The third strategy, then, is to set clearly stated, worthwhile, reachable goals for our lives that are worthy of our commitment and that will demand our best effort.

Strategy #4 is to *sharpen our focus*. After establishing our goals, each of us must then focus our attention on those goals. That was probably the secret of Albert Einstein's success. Of course, he was a brilliant man, but perhaps the secret of his success went beyond his intelligence, as is demonstrated in his strange response to a simple question someone asked him one day. When someone asked Einstein what his phone number was, Einstein went to the phone book to look it up. In shock, the other man said, "Do you mean you don't even know what your own phone number is?" Einstein replied, "No, I never clutter my mind with information I can find somewhere else!"[4]

Sometimes our minds are so cluttered with things to remember and our lives are so ensnared with things to do that we get bogged down, for this clutter demotivates us. Motivated people are people who know what they want to do and then concentrate their attention on that priority. To be motivated to get out of bed every morning, every Christian will have to say "No" to some less important demands in order to say "Yes" to the most important demands. The fourth strategy, then, is to establish a plan that will enable us to focus on the priorities. In the words of a popular expression, it means to make the main thing the main thing.

Final Word

Many challenges face us every day of our lives, but perhaps the greatest challenge is the challenge to get started. The Scriptures cited above, the model of the Apostle Paul, and the specific strategies identified can all serve as gadgets to get us started as we navigate around this particular roadblock that often keeps us from experiencing the full and abundant life God makes available to us through Jesus Christ.

Prayer

Father God
Who guides
Both our starts
And our stops
We ask for your help.

Kindle a fire
In our soul and
Create a vision
In our heart.

Get the lead
Out of our seat
And put some life
Into our feet.

Give us the courage
To face the day
And give us the faith
To claim it for you.

Amen.

NOTES

[1] John Killinger, "Gratitude Makes the Difference," in *Great Preaching 1989*, ed. Michael Duduit (Jacksonville FL: The Preaching Library, 1989), 20-21.

[2] *Quote* 51: 13.

[3] Dolly Parton, *Dolly* (New York: HarperCollins Publishers, 1994), 78.

[4] Kenneth Blanchard and Spencer Johnson, *The One Minute Manager* (New York: Berkley Books, 1981), 70.

When We Have to Choose

The Indecisiveness Roadblock

He'd been warned that Gerber was something of a dullard, but the postmaster decided to hire him anyway. It was Christmas and he needed an extra set of hands to sort the mail. On Gerber's first day of sorting the mail, much to everyone's surprise, he separated the letters so fast that his motions were literally a blur. At the end of the day, the postmaster said to Gerber, "I want you to know how proud I am of you. You're one of the fastest workers we've ever had." "Thank you, sir," Gerber replied, "and tomorrow I'll try to do even better." "Better?" the postmaster said in astonishment. "How can you do any better?" Gerber explained, "Tomorrow I'm going to read the addresses."

Choosing was easy for Gerber! However, for most of us, making choices is a much more difficult undertaking. Because of the multiplicity of options before us today, making choices is more difficult than ever before. Unable to decide what we want to do, we are often unmade by our unmade decisions. The dilemma of making choices becomes another roadblock that keeps us from enjoying the abundant life Jesus wants us to experience. Steering around this roadblock means liberating ourselves to make the right decisions in our lives at the right time.

Search the Scripture

For the Christian, the place to begin in seeking answers is the Scripture. Several Scriptures provide instruction for being more decisive in our choices. Let me list a few of them.

- Psalm 119:97-100: "Oh, how I love your law! I meditate on it all day long. Your commands make me wiser than my enemies, for they are ever with me. I have more insight than all my teachers, for I meditate on your statutes. I have more understanding than the elders, for I obey your precepts."
- Proverbs 3:5-6: "Trust in the LORD with all your heart and lean not on your own understanding; in all your ways acknowledge him, and he will make your paths straight."
- Proverbs 13:20: "He who walks with the wise grows wise, but a companion of fools suffers harm."
- Proverbs 15:22: "Plans fail for lack of counsel, but with many advisers they succeed."
- John 16:13: "But when he, the Spirit of truth, comes, he will guide you into all truth. He will not speak on his own; he will speak only what he hears, and he will tell you what is yet to come."
- Philippians 4:6-7: "Do not be anxious about anything, but in everything, by prayer and petition, with thanksgiving, present your requests to God. And the peace of God, which transcends all understanding, will guard your hearts and your minds in Christ Jesus."

To begin with, these Scriptures reaffirm the importance of God's word in making our decisions. The insights and instructions in the Bible provide guidance for the Christian who wants to make the right choices. According to Psalm 19, knowledge of God's word will enable us to walk in God's way. Even Jesus used God's word as the basis for choosing the right response to Satan, for he confronted each of Satan's temptations in the wilderness with the phrase, "For it is written . . . ," and then he quoted a Scripture as a rationale for his decision (Matt 4:4, 6, 7, 10). Likewise, for us, listening to God's word will enable us to walk more effectively in God's way.

These Scriptures also underscore the importance of faith in making the right decisions. Not just through his word but also through his presence in our lives, God will help us make the right decisions if we will listen to him and trust him. That is the advice of one of the best-known passages from the Old Testament, Proverbs 3:5-6. Some people say, "I would be glad to do what God wants me to do if he would just tell me. I listen to God, but I don't hear him speaking to me. How can I know what God wants me to do?" The answer to those questions is found in the word "acknowledge" (Prov 3:6). To acknowledge God is to become aware of who he is. To acknowledge God is to fellowship with him in prayer and Bible study and corporate worship. To acknowledge God is to come to know him. When we do that, the writer of Proverbs says, "He will direct your paths."

Further, these Scriptures point out the influence of our peers in making the proper choices. Proverbs 13:20 and 15:22 both remind us of the importance of our peer group. Of course, our peer group can either help us or hurt us. If they are wise, they can enrich our lives. If they are foolish, they can increase the suffering of our lives. In either case, they will inevitably influence us. Thus, seeking wise counsel is an important step in decision-making. In his book *A Pretty Good Person,* author Lewis B. Smedes expresses this truth: "Because our discernment is *always*—not sometimes, but always—partial, we need communities of shared discernment."[1] Being part of a community of shared discernment will enable us to make wiser choices.

These Scriptures also reinforce the contribution of the Holy Spirit in making the decisions of our lives. For example, John 16:13 reminds us that every Christian has the indwelling Spirit whose purpose is to guide us in the direction God wants us to go. Choosing our outward company is not always possible, for life often forces us into communities not of our choosing. Sometimes our outward company is determined by the circumstances of our lives—our living space or our context at work. However, each of us can choose to enjoy the spiritual companionship of the indwelling Holy Spirit.

Finally, these Scriptures remind us of the importance of prayer in our decision-making. The powerful promise concerning prayer in Paul's letter to the Philippians reminds us of the importance of prayer in the decision-making process. In response to our prayer, God will both guard us and guide us (Phil 4:6-7). In a scene in the movie *Shadowlands,* Anthony Hopkins, who plays the part of C. S. Lewis, says, "Prayer doesn't change God. It changes me!" That can be true of every Christian. Through the ears of our heart, prayer speaks the directions of God that steer us in the way God wants us to go.

God's word is packed with informative insights for Christians who want to move around the roadblock of indecisiveness. In addition, many characters introduced to us in Scripture flesh out these insights in their lives. The Bible is full of models of those who were incisive in making decisions, but I want to focus on the man we know as Gideon (Judg 6–7). He lived in Israel at a time when God's people were oppressed by the Midianites, a period when the nation of Israel was contaminated by the worship of Baal. God called Gideon to overthrow the Midianites and to destroy the altars that had been constructed for the worship of Baal. Several steps marked Gideon's decision-making process.

Step one was *to recognize the need.* Gideon clearly understood that Israel had a problem, for the promises of God had clearly not been fulfilled (Judg 6:13). Through an encounter with the angel of God, Gideon became aware of the cause of the problem in Israel and discovered what needed to be done to solve the problem (6:14-24).

Step two was *to enlist the help.* Gideon was hesitant to tackle the challenge alone, so he selected ten men to assist him in tearing down the altar of Baal (6:27). He then gathered the troops of Israel and selected three hundred men to assist him in his battle against the Midianites (6:34-35).

Step three was *to make certain he had God's support.* He accomplished this by the laying out of the fleece (6:36-40). On the one hand, he seemed a little slow on the uptake. On the other hand, the positive side of Gideon's action is that he wanted to make sure he was doing what God wanted him to do.

Step four was *to develop a strategy* that would enable him to accomplish his goal (7:15-18). Through the direct word from the Lord and through the indirect word of a dream, Gideon developed a plan. Then he told his three-hundred-man army, "Watch me. Follow my lead. When I get to the edge of the camp, do exactly as I do" (7:17). Recognition, support, caution, strategy—these were all a part of Gideon's plan for making the proper choices. Studying his story closely in Judges 6–7 will enable us to make decisions more effectively today.

Set the Strategy

From Gideon's model and from the clear teachings of Scripture, Christians in today's world can shape strategies for making the right decisions at the right time. Let me suggest several strategies.

Strategy #1 is to *refine our focus.* Alvin Toffler wrote a watershed book about change in 1970 titled *Future Shock.* He introduced a word that captures the experience of each of us today—"overchoice." When we buy an ice cream, we have dozens of flavors from which to choose. When we watch television, we have hundreds of channels to watch. When we buy an automobile, our choices are even more overwhelming. In his 1970 book, Toffler told of a computer specialist who put into his computer all the variations available in automobiles—body styles, colors, accessories, etc. The computer suggested 25 million different combinations![2] That was in 1970. Imagine the combinations available today! With such a plethora of choices, the place to begin in our plan for making proper choices is to refine the focus of our lives on the decisions that can be made and that should be made.

Lincoln Kirstein, founder of the New York City Ballet and School, provides an extreme example of this strategy. He wore the same clothes every day, and here is his reasoning: "I long ago worked out that I would save a great deal of time if I forewent the particular choice of dress."[3] In similar but perhaps less dramatic ways, each of us can narrow our choices by refining our focus.

Strategy #2 is to *clarify our options.* After refining our focus and identifying the decisions that have to be made, the next step is to study each decision to make sure we understand our options. The waitress who would ask her customers each morning, "Do you want one egg or two?" caused some of the customers to lose sight of the possibility that they might not want any eggs at all or that they might not want any breakfast at all. Making the right decision is not possible until we clearly understand all the options we have. Only then can we make the right choice at the right time.

Strategy #3 is to *establish some guidelines.* To make the right choices at the right time also requires guidelines by which the correct option can be determined. Different suggestions have been offered as to the proper guidelines for making the right choices.

For example, well-known pastor John Claypool once said that he passed his decisions through the net of three questions: the limits question, the gifts question, and the obedience question. The limits question asked, "Given the pool of psychic, physical, spiritual, and intellectual energy I possess, which is the decision that I can accomplish?" The gifts question asked, "Which decision is in line with the shape of my own uniqueness?" The obedience question asked, "What does God's will dictate?"[4] That is one possible set of guidelines.

Author Leslie B. Flynn offers another set of guidelines by suggesting three additional questions to ask before making a decision. Question one: Which decision will glorify God? Question two: Which decision will bless others? And question three: Which decision will help me? These three questions can also guide us as we make our decisions.[5]

For me personally, I have established a mission statement for my life that I regularly review and daily remember. Especially when an important decision has to be made, I will examine the alternatives before me under the microscope of my personal mission statement. Whatever guidelines you adopt, the point remains: every Christian needs guidelines. This is a crucial part of the decision-making process.

Strategy #4 is to *consider the consequences.* Every choice has consequences. Sometimes a choice seems appealing until we chart out the consequences of that choice. Remember again the experience of David. David chose to go to bed with Bathsheba (2 Sam 11). It seemed like a good idea at the time. However, David did not consider the consequences of that action—Bathsheba's pregnancy, the necessity for the eventual elimination of Uriah, the death of the baby born out of this indiscretion, the loss of the respect of his children, and eventually the disintegration of his family. Had he considered the consequences he might have made a different choice.

Anticipating the future is of course a tricky process. Trying to determine exactly where a decision today will put us tomorrow is problematic. Nevertheless, taking the long look when choosing what to do is a vital step in making the right decisions at the right time.

Strategy #5 is to *seek counsel.* Biblical admonition and human experience coincide at this point. Both confirm the importance of getting advice from others before important decisions are made. Sometimes a friend will raise questions that have evaded our notice. Sometimes our colleagues can point out consequences that have escaped our perception. Sometimes they will suggest options we have not even considered. Sometimes they can share out of an experience we have not yet had. In any of these manifestations, the wise counsel of others will be beneficial in our decision-making process.

Strategy #6 is to *be willing to adjust.* Because no one is perfect, no one will be perfect in the choices he makes. Even with the most thoughtful approach to making decisions and even after seeking the best advice, we will still make mistakes and wrong decisions. In those instances, we must be willing to adjust.

Christians often attribute greater value to being consistent than to being right. Some suggest that it is courageous to stick with a decision once it is made and to fight for it to the end. Actually, it is both more courageous and more Christian to say, "I made that decision, but it was the wrong decision. Based on further light, I am now moving in a different direction." When our decisions confirm our commitment to Christ and the guidelines established for decision-making in our lives, consistency is called for. However, when our decisions push us toward consequences that weaken our commitment to Christ and negatively affect the lives of those around us, changing our mind is both the most courageous and Christian thing to do.

Final Word

No one can escape the responsibility of making choices. Decision-making is an inevitable part of living. Even refusing to choose is a choice. Choices are inevitable in the process of living. Therefore, trying to avoid making decisions is not the proper approach for the Christian. Instead, Christians need to establish strategies that will enable them to navigate around this roadblock and move toward the abundant life God has provided for us in Jesus Christ.

Prayer

Dear Heavenly Father
We look to you for help
In making the decisions
Of our lives.

We can't see far enough or
Understand clearly enough
To make the right choices
On our own.

Sharpen our vision and
Stimulate our minds
So we can see your way and

Understand your word and
Follow your will.

Amen.

NOTES

[1] Lewis B. Smedes, *A Pretty Good Person* (San Francisco: Harper & Row, 1990), 144.

[2] Alvin Toffler, *Future Shock* (New York: Random House, 1970), 230.

[3] Warren Bennis and Burt Nanus, *Leaders* (New York: Harper & Row, 1985), 31.

[4] John R. Claypool, "Saying Yes and Saying No," sermon preached at Northminster Baptist Church in Jackson MI, 26 February 1978.

[5] Leslie B. Flynn, *How to Save Time in the Ministry* (Grand Rapids MI: Baker Book House, 1966), 38.

When We Feel All Alone

The Loneliness Roadblock

I don't remember all the details of the story the preacher told years ago, but the part I do remember haunts me. A certain woman was eighty-five years old, and the people in the nursing home called her Miss Victoria. She had no family and apparently no friends. No one ever came to visit her. One day, a man from a local church was visiting someone who was in the room next to Miss Victoria. He noticed her coming out of her room, stopped to speak to her, and ended up visiting with her. This began a series of visits to Miss Victoria. After a few weeks, she told her new friend, "I have a favor to ask. I would really like to kiss someone before I die and I wonder if you would be that someone."

The word "loneliness" describes Miss Victoria's situation. Webster defines loneliness as "unhappy being alone." Ironically, the word "loneliness" does not appear in the Bible. In fact, it was not until recent times that this word was even a part of our vocabulary. The Oxford English Dictionary dates the use of the English word "lonely" in the sense of "sad at being alone" to a line in a poem written by Byron in 1811. The noun "loneliness" did not appear in any major dictionary until after World War II.[1]

Although it is a fairly recent term, loneliness is nevertheless an ancient and universal problem. It is one of the most serious roadblocks on the highway of life. Paul Tournier calls loneliness "the most devastating malady of this age."[2] And Mother Teresa called it "the leprosy of the west."[3] Loneliness often becomes a roadblock that prevents us from being what God wants us to be and doing what God wants us to do. If we are to experience the abundant life God wants us to experience, we will have to learn how to get around this roadblock.

Search the Scripture

For the Christian, the place to begin in seeking answers is the word of God. Even though the word "loneliness" does not appear in the Bible, a number of passages address the issue of loneliness. Let me list a few of them.

- Genesis 2:18: "The LORD God said, 'It is not good for the man to be alone. I will make a helper suitable for him.'"
- Deuteronomy 31:8: "The LORD himself goes before you and will be with you; he will never leave you nor forsake you."
- Joshua 1:9: "Do not be terrified; do not be discouraged, for the LORD your God will be with you wherever you go."
- Psalm 16:8b: "Because he is so near, I never need to stumble or to fall" (TLB).
- Psalm 23:4: "Even though I walk through the valley of the shadow of death, I will fear no evil, for you are with me."
- Psalm 46:10: "Be still, and know that I am God."
- Psalm 139:7-10: "Where can I go from your Spirit? Where can I flee from your presence? If I go up to the heavens, you are there; if I make my bed in the depths, you are there. If I rise on the wings of the dawn, if I settle on the far side of the sea, even there your hand will guide me, your right hand will hold me fast."
- Isaiah 43:2: "When you pass through the waters, I will be with you."
- Matthew 28:20b: "And surely I am with you always, to the very end of the age."
- Mark 8:35: "For whoever wants to save his life will lose it, but whoever loses his life for me and for the gospel will save it."
- Hebrews 12:1-2: "Therefore, since we are surrounded by such a great cloud of witnesses, let us throw off everything that hinders and the sin that so

easily entangles, and let us run with perseverance the race marked out for us. Let us fix our eyes on Jesus, the author and perfecter of our faith."

First, these Scriptures assure us that we are never really alone. In every place and during every day of our lives, God is with us, even if his presence is not apparent. As Barbara Brown Taylor explains, "Sometimes God's hand is so obvious you can see it for miles; at other times, you have to dust for fingerprints."[4] Nevertheless, God's word assures us of God's presence in our lives at all times (Ps 139:7-10). Because of the constant companionship of God, a Christian is never really alone.

In addition to God's presence, Christians also have the support of the other members of the family of God. Christians are part of a tradition that includes thousands of others in days past and that will include thousands of others in the days ahead who are part of God's forever family along with us. As the writer of Hebrews puts it, "We are surrounded by such a great cloud of witnesses" (12:1). Because of the connection with the saints across the ages, a Christian is never really alone.

Second, these Scriptures remind us of the value of our times of physical aloneness. These times alone can in fact be constructive times of growth if we respond to them in the proper way. Sometimes, only by withdrawing from our physical contact with others can we make spiritual contact with God. That idea is expressed in Psalm 46:10: "Be still, and know that I am God." And that is the truth captured in the pattern of Jesus described in Matthew 14:23: "After he had dismissed them, he went up on a mountainside by himself to pray. When evening came, he was there alone." Sometimes physical aloneness provides the context for deepening our relationship with God.

Further, these Scriptures reveal the danger of loneliness. God created us for relationships as the creation account in Genesis clearly affirms (2:18). Yet sometimes God's presence cannot be detected in the ebb and flow of our lives. Even though our times of physical aloneness can be constructive times of growth, they often are not. Instead, the loneliness can wreak havoc with our sense of personal worth. When sixteen-year-old Robin Graham, accompanied only by two kittens, sailed around the world on his 24-foot sloop *Dove*, he found loneliness to be his greatest obstacle. "Loneliness," he later wrote, "was to grip me for a thousand days and nights. At times it was almost as if loneliness had climbed aboard *Dove* with cold, clammy hands that reached out for my throat and heart—and stomach. Loneliness was to be an enemy that I never quite managed to conquer."[5] Loneliness struck Robin

Graham in his times of physical aloneness. On the other hand, even when we are surrounded by people, loneliness still can strike at the foundation of our lives and become a roadblock that keeps us from enjoying the abundant life Jesus wants us to experience.

The suggestions from the Scriptures to remember the presence of God, to reach out to our connections with other Christians, and to use the times of physical aloneness to cultivate our soul provide a place to begin in navigating around this roadblock of loneliness. Further lessons can be discerned from the men and women of the Bible who fleshed out these truths in their lives. One of the best biblical models of effectively dealing with loneliness is the prophet Elijah. In 1 Kings 18, Elijah triumphed in his conflict against the gods of Baal and Asherah. What a high moment in his life! But then, in 1 Kings 19, we see Elijah hiding in a cave, totally removed from other people, in the depths of depression. God comes to Elijah and says, "What are you doing here?" (v. 9). Elijah explains his condition in a single sentence: "I am the only one left" (v. 10). Loneliness had overwhelmed Elijah. How did God respond? God told Elijah to stand before the mountain. Then God spoke to him in the quietness of the gentle breeze.

Still, this was not enough to break Elijah out of his loneliness, so Elijah retired again to the cave. Once again God asked him, "What are you doing here?" (v. 13). Again, Elijah responded with the note of despair, "I alone am left" (v. 14). God then told Elijah to leave the cave, to return to his fellow countrymen, and to give himself in service to God and his country. As a final word of encouragement, God reminded Elijah that he was not in fact alone but that seven thousand others had remained faithful and were ready to serve God (v. 18). So Elijah left the cave, moved past the temporary roadblock of loneliness, and began once more to serve God.

Elijah demonstrates all three lessons spelled out above. He felt the devastation of loneliness. Then he discovered that he was not really alone. Finally, he used his time of physical aloneness as a time of personal growth. He provides a model for effectively moving around the roadblock of loneliness.

Set the Strategy

These principles modeled by Elijah in the experience narrated in 1 Kings 18–19 provide a pool of resources from which to develop strategies for facing loneliness in our lives. Here are some possible strategies to get us started.

Strategy #1 is to *practice the presence of God.* A family moved to a new community, and on the first Sunday they got into the car and drove to a church a couple of blocks from their house. On their way home, the little girl said to her parents, "You know, we're lucky to live in the same neighborhood as God." Scripture after Scripture confirm the truth of that little girl's pronouncement, for we do have the privilege of living in the same neighborhood as God. In fact, according to the Bible, God is not only with us; he is also within us (John 14:23).

One of the antidotes for loneliness then is to cultivate a relationship with God through prayer and meditation, to practice the presence of God. This is probably what Paul had in mind when he admonished us to "pray without ceasing" (1 Thess 5:7). To be constantly focused on God, constantly aware of God's presence, constantly talking to God, and constantly listening for God—these are the characteristics of a Christian who prays without ceasing. Incorporating these characteristics into our lives will enable us to practice the presence of God each day.

Strategy #2 is to *develop a proper understanding of loneliness.* It is important for us to realize that loneliness is not the same thing as aloneness. Aloneness is physical; loneliness is psychological. It is possible to be alone and not be lonely. It is also possible to be lonely and not be alone. Henry David Thoreau once defined city life as a million people being lonesome together.[5] Recognizing the distinction between these two words will help us develop a proper understanding of loneliness.

Likewise, it is important for us to realize that loneliness is not the same thing as solitude. Loneliness is a negative psychological condition. On the other hand, solitude can be positive. One man contrasted the two different realities in this way: "Loneliness speaks of the pain of being alone; solitude expresses the glory of being alone."[6] Recognizing the distinction between these two words will also help us develop a proper understanding of loneliness.

Understanding is crucial at this point. Lack of clarity about the distinction between aloneness and loneliness will lead us to expend our energies making sure people are around us instead of expending our energies on actually making connection with these people. Further, lack of clarity about the distinction between loneliness and solitude might cause us to give so much attention to dispelling our loneliness that we miss opportunities for personal growth in times of solitude. Thus, it is important for us to develop a proper understanding of loneliness.

Strategy #3 is to *do something for others*. Because loneliness often comes from an internal focus, one strategy for dealing with loneliness is to change the focus of our lives. That is why Jesus' statement in Mark 8:35—to save our lives by losing them—should be an essential part of our strategy for dealing with loneliness. An internal focus that comes from our desire to save our lives must be replaced by an external focus that inspires us to give our lives away. Tim Hansel says it well: "Mirrors and windows are both made of glass, but they serve two distinctly different purposes. A window allows you to see out, to see the world, to see others, to get a perspective on life. A mirror focuses on your preoccupation with yourself. What we have got to do with our loneliness is to change our mirrors to windows."[7]

Looking at a mirror only brings to our attention a vision of ourselves. In contrast, looking through the window enables us to see others. Therefore, spending more time looking through windows rather than looking into mirrors is another strategy for overcoming loneliness.

Strategy #4 is to *remember our connectedness*. From the earliest days of the church the idea of individuality was mediated by the sense of community among those who shared the Christian faith. In other words, through Christ the Christian is not only brought into a relationship with God. The Christian is also brought into a relationship with other Christians. This "sense of community" shows up all the way through the New Testament. The New Testament says a Christian is part of a body (Eph 4:16); belongs to a flock (1 Pet 5:2); is among the ecclesia, the called-out ones (Col 1:18); and is a member of God's family (Gal 6:10).

Whenever loneliness grips our lives, Christians should remember our connectedness. Every one of us is part of that great cloud of witnesses that includes Abraham and Moses and David in the past and that will include unnamed men and women in the future. The antidote for loneliness then is not only to recognize and develop our connectedness with God but also to recognize and develop our connectedness with each other.

Final Word

Everybody is alone at times. In fact, everybody needs to be alone at times, for sometimes, only by being alone can we develop ourselves effectively. And sometimes, only by being alone with God can we get to know him in a more intimate way. However, loneliness, as I have pointed out, is a different matter. Therefore, to keep our "aloneness" from deteriorating into "loneliness"—"the sense of being unhappy being alone"—here are strategies to put into place in our lives: practice the presence of God, develop a proper understanding of loneliness, do something for someone else, and remember our connectedness.

Prayer

Dear omnipresent God,
We do not ask
That you be present with us
For we are never
Out of your presence.

Help us instead
To recognize your presence and
To revel in your presence,
For in knowing you better
We know ourselves better.

Forgive us when we ask you
To remove the very thing
You may be using
To make us more like you.

Amen.

NOTES

[1] As noted in John Haggai, *How To Win Over Loneliness* (Nashville: Thomas Nelson, 1979), 20.

[2] Gary Collins, *Overcoming Anxiety* (Santa Ana CA: Vision House Publishers, 1973), 121.

[3] Navin Chawla, *Mother Teresa* (Rockport MA: Element, 1992), xix.

[4] Barbara Brown Taylor, *Gospel Medicine* (Cambridge: Cowley Publications, 1995), 120.

[5] Quoted by Edward Paul Cohn, "This Thing Called . . . Loneliness," *Pulpit Digest* (May-June, 1986): 53.

[6] Collins, *Overcoming Anxiety,* 125.

[7] Tim Hansel, *Through the Wilderness of Loneliness* (Elgin IL: David C. Cook, 1991), 126.

When We Think Too Highly of Ourselves

The Pride Roadblock

Savanarola, a Florentine preacher of the fifteenth century, observed an elderly woman worshiping at the statue of the Virgin Mary in the city's great cathedral. The next day, he saw her again before the statue of Mary, on her knees in obvious adoration. When the pattern continued, Savanarola commented to one of his fellow priests, "Look how she reverences the Virgin Mother." The other priest responded, "It's not what you think. Many years ago an artist was commissioned to create a statue for the cathedral. He found a lovely young woman to be his model for the statue. The woman who now worships the statue is the same one who served as its model years ago. Shortly after the statue was put in place, she began to visit it and has continued to do so ever since."[1] The woman was not worshiping God; she was worshiping herself.

In less obvious ways, many of us also worship ourselves. This tendency to think too highly of ourselves—we call it pride—is one of the major roadblocks to productive daily living. Developing a strategy for moving around this roadblock is an essential step in experiencing the abundant life God wants us to experience.

Search the Scripture

For the Christian, the place to begin in seeking answers is the Scripture. A number of verses in the Bible address this particular roadblock. Let me identify a few of them.

- Deuteronomy 8:18: "But remember the LORD your God, for it is he who gives you the ability to produce wealth, and so confirms his covenant, which he swore to your forefathers, as it is today."
- Psalm 101:5b: "Whoever has haughty eyes and a proud heart, him will I not endure."
- Proverbs 16:5: "The LORD detests all the proud of heart. Be sure of this: They will not go unpunished."
- Proverbs 16:18: "Pride goes before destruction, a haughty spirit before a fall."
- Ecclesiastes 4:9-12: "Two are better than one, because they have a good return for their work: If one falls down, his friend can help him up. But pity the man who falls and has no one to help him up! Also, if two lie down together, they will keep warm. But how can one keep warm alone? Though one may be overpowered, two can defend themselves."
- Romans 12:3: "Do not think of yourself more highly than you ought, but rather think of yourself with sober judgment, in accordance with the measure of faith God has given you."
- 1 Corinthians 4:7: "What do you have that you did not receive?"
- 1 Corinthians 10:12: "So, if you think you are standing firm, be careful that you don't fall!"
- Galatians 6:3: "If anyone thinks he is something when he is nothing, he deceives himself."
- Philippians 2:3: "Do nothing out of selfish ambition or vain conceit, but in humility consider others better than yourselves."
- James 1:17: "Every good and perfect gift is from above, coming down from the Father of the heavenly lights, who does not change like shifting shadows."
- James 4:6: "God opposes the proud but gives grace to the humble."

To begin with, these Scriptures remind us of the dominance of pride. The Bible has more to say about pride than most of the other roadblocks considered in this book, because pride is a universal problem in human life. When C. S. Lewis called pride "the central vice"[2] and when author Patrick Morley called pride "the patriarch of man's sins,"[3] they were standing on firm scriptural ground. In the Bible, pride is one of the most often cited issues.

Biographer Graham Lord detailed how pride threatened to disrupt the life of James Herriot, the country vet who rose to worldwide fame through his phenomenally successful books, including international bestseller *All Creatures Great and Small*. Herriot's awkwardness in his early speaking engagements was quickly replaced by a confidence that evolved dangerously close to pride. When a friend remarked about his amazing confidence as a speaker, Herriot replied in his rich Scots brogue, "Aye, Dick, it's a heady brew and I'm giving it up." He never spoke publicly again because he recognized how easily pride could raise its ugly head and twist him into something he did not want to be.[4]

In addition, these Scriptures reflect the deception of pride. According to the Bible, everything in life is a gift (Jas 1:17). No one is a "self-made" person. Our lives find their source and strength in God. Pride is deceptive because it causes us to exaggerate our standing in relationship to God (1 Cor 4:7; Gal 6:3). Jesus captured the problem in his story about a religious leader in his day who was puffed up with pride (Luke 18:9-14). This man went to the temple one day to pray, and his prayer was full of himself: "I thank you that I am not like other men." He went on to pray, "I fast twice a week and give a tenth of all I get" (Luke 18:11-12). This man evidently thought a lot of himself. But Jesus' clearest indictment of the man's pride comes in the introduction to the man's prayer. Jesus says, "The Pharisee stood up and prayed *about* himself" (Luke 18:11). Some translations say he prayed "*to*" himself. This man was obviously confused about who was God!

Pride not only causes us to exaggerate our standing in relationship to God. It also causes us to exaggerate our standing in relationship to other people. No one is an island. Our lives are interconnected with others and are dependent upon others. Pride is deceptive because it blinds us to our dependence on other people (Eccl 4:9-12). An apocryphal story about President Theodore Roosevelt's first day in heaven demonstrates this problem. Teddy Roosevelt was known for his bombastic spirit and exuberant confidence. Apparently, this carried over to his encounter with St. Peter when he arrived in heaven. Teddy Roosevelt marched up to St. Peter and complained, "This heavenly choir is inexcusably weak! We must reorganize it at once." Consequently, St. Peter enlisted the newcomer in heaven to carry out the reorganization. So Teddy told St. Peter, "I'll need ten thousand sopranos, ten thousand altos, and ten thousand tenors." Peter replied, "But what about the basses?" And Teddy retorted, "I'll sing bass!" Like the former president as depicted in this tale (and often in real life as well), we often exaggerate our importance in relationship to the other people in our lives. Paul's word of warning to the Galatian Christians should be a reminder to us whenever pride sets in: "If anyone thinks he is something when he is nothing, he deceives himself" (Gal 6:3).

These Scriptures also reveal the danger of pride. Pride is often the prelude to deception and disaster. This truth is captured in Proverbs 16:18: "Pride goes before destruction, a haughty spirit before a fall." Paul echoes the same idea in 1 Corinthians 10:12. Aesop illustrated the danger of pride in his fable about the mice who decided they needed to be better organized. Some were elected leaders, and for a while the organization helped. After some time, however, the leaders got caught up in their own self-importance. They noted their leadership by wearing special uniforms with lots of medals and tall hats so everyone could recognize them as leaders. But one day the cat launched a surprise attack and the mice ran for their lives. Unfortunately, the mice leaders were so weighted down by their heavy medals that they could not run fast. Even more unfortunately, when they reached the escape hatch, they could not get in because their hats were too tall. The cat enjoyed a sumptuous feast, made possible because of the haughty spirit of the mice leaders, the kind of spirit the Bible says always goes before a fall.[5]

Memorizing the Scriptures cited above is a starting place for navigating around the roadblock of pride. Further instruction can come from those in the Bible who model the proper way to avoid the onslaught of pride. One of the most intriguing examples of a person who refused to think too highly of himself but instead recognized that everything he had came from God was the Old Testament prophet Daniel.

The first chapter of Daniel describes the prophet as a young man of incredible qualities and extraordinary achievements. Daniel 1:15 describes Daniel and his three buddies in these words: "At the end of the ten days they looked healthier and better nourished than any of the young men who ate the royal food." Daniel 1:20 adds, "In every matter of wisdom and understanding about which the king questioned them, he found them ten times better than all the magicians and enchanters in his whole kingdom." Daniel and his companions stood head and shoulders above the other young leaders. Then the king had a dream and was anxious for someone to interpret it. Daniel and his friends prayed that God would reveal the meaning of the dream to them. Daniel 2:19 says, "During the night the mystery was revealed to Daniel in a vision." This was heady stuff for young Daniel, being elevated above the other young men in training, hobnobbing with the king, and receiving special revelations from God.

How easy it would have been for Daniel to begin saying, "Look at what I have done." Instead, the Bible says Daniel "blessed the God of heaven" with this prayer:

> Praise be to the name of God for ever and ever; wisdom and power are his. He changes times and seasons; he sets up kings and deposes them. He gives wisdom to the wise and knowledge to the discerning. He reveals deep and hidden things; he knows what lies in darkness, and light dwells with him. I thank and praise you, O God of my fathers: You have given me wisdom and power, you have made known to me what we asked of you, you have made known to us the dream of the king. (Dan 2:20-23)

Daniel could have thought highly of himself. Instead, he thought highly of God because he recognized that all he had came from God. Daniel modeled the proper attitude we should have toward ourselves if we are to avoid the roadblock of pride.

Set the Strategy

From these Scriptures and from the example of Daniel, certain insights can be drawn that will provide the framework for a strategic approach to the danger of pride.

Strategy #1 is to *distinguish between positive pride and negative pride.* Webster includes both a positive and negative definition for pride. The first definition for pride is "an overly high opinion of oneself." That is negative pride, and it is obviously an attitude to avoid. Most of the verses cited above speak to this negative kind of pride. However, another of Webster's definitions for pride is "a sense of one's own dignity; self-respect." That is positive pride, and it is an attitude to inculcate into our lives. Romans 8:15 speaks of this positive kind of pride:

> For you did not receive a spirit that makes you a slave again to
> fear, but you received the Spirit of sonship. And by him we cry,
> *"Abba,* Father." The Spirit himself testifies with our spirit that we
> are God's children. Now if we are children, then we are heirs—
> heirs of God and co-heirs with Christ, if indeed we share in his
> sufferings in order that we may also share in his glory.

Pride in our own accomplishments is to be avoided, but pride in our
birthright as children of God is to be embraced.

The key then is to distinguish between these two kinds of pride.
Otherwise, we will expend a great deal of energy trying to subdue the
healthy sense of self-respect that should be embraced because of our
birthright as children of God. Denying our position as God's children is not
the right step. Denying our power through Christ that will enable us to do
all things through him is not the right step (Phil 4:13). These things should
not be subdued; they should be embraced, for they remind us whose we are.
Then, knowing *whose* we are will lead to a healthy respect for *who* we are.
This is a good kind of pride. Distinguishing this good kind of pride from the
negative, destructive kind of pride in order to focus our attention on the real
problem—negative pride—is a key strategy in moving around this roadblock.

Strategy #2 is to *remember where we came from.* Perhaps President Harry
Truman provides one of the clearest examples of a person who never forgot
where he came from. Harry Truman had been vice president for only eighty-
three days when Franklin Delano Roosevelt died on April 12, 1945. Truman
happened to be at the right place at the right time and ended up as the
thirty-third president of the United States. Earlier, Truman dreamed of being
a concert pianist, but the lack of money brought his training to an end. He
also wanted to go to the military academy at West Point, but his eyesight
would not allow it. He went into the clothing business in Kansas City, but
the business failed. In the 1944 election, he became a compromise candidate
for vice president and then, with Roosevelt's death, became an accidental
president. Truman made quite an ascent from Independence, Missouri, to
the White House. Consequently, Truman could have thought highly of himself. He countered this temptation to pride with a simple strategy. "I tried
never to forget who I was and where I'd come from."[6]

On a tour to a certain city, one of the tourists asked the guide, "Were
any great men born here?" "No," said the guide, "only babies." No matter

what a person accomplishes, he is still simply a person like all others, created by God. Whenever our ego begins to be pumped up by an exalted view of ourselves, the key is to remember where we came from.

Strategy #3 is to *remember where we are going*. No matter how much success has come our way here on earth, every person will discover death to be the great equalizer, for it comes to all people, no matter what their level of achievement or what financial accumulation they have made. Death brings to each of us to a time of accountability before God.

The Old Testament story of King Belshazzar of Babylon reveals this inevitable accountability (Dan 5). Belshazzar hosted a state banquet for his nobles. In drunken bravado he decided to raise a toast to the gods of Babylon by using the goblets confiscated from the temple in Jerusalem. Their drunken toast was interrupted by the bazaar appearance of a human hand, writing a message on the wall. The king called for his wise men to interpret the message, but none of them could do it. Finally, the prophet Daniel was called in. Before interpreting this message of judgment on Belshazzar, Daniel explained the reason for it. Recalling the experience of the former king Nebuchadnezzar being humbled by the decree of Yahweh, Daniel told the young king that he should have remembered what these experiences had taught his grandfather about humility and respect for the Lord. Instead, Belshazzar's blasphemous pride led him to profane the Lord's holy vessels in his drunken orgy. As a result, God's message for the king, scribbled by the hand on the wall, spelled out Belshazzar's imminent doom.

Like Belshazzar, each of us must ultimately give an account of our lives to God. Consequently, whenever an exalted opinion of ourselves begins to take hold of us, the key is to remember where we are going. The reminder of our ultimate accountability to God should cause us to live humbly before the Lord who created us, who has redeemed us through his Son, and who has empowered us through his Spirit.

Final Word

English writer and theologian G. K. Chesterton once said, "If I had only one sermon to preach it would be against pride."[7] G. K. Chesterton recognized that pride is one of the roadblocks that keeps us from experiencing the full and abundant life for which Jesus saved us. The strategies cited above provide a starting place for navigating around this roadblock.

Prayer

Supreme God and Creator
How awesome is your name.
We glory in your greatness.

How easily we forget
That everything we have
Comes from you.

And even the ability to obtain
What we have
Comes from you.

Remind us
who you are and
whose we are
So that we will never
Be confused
About who we are.

Amen.

NOTES

[1] As described in Anthony Campolo, *Seven Deadly Sins* (Wheaton IL: Victor Books, 1987), 74.

[2] C. S. Lewis, *Mere Christianity* (New York: Macmillan Publishing Co., 1943), 94.

[3] Patrick Morley, *The Man in the Mirror* (Brentwood TN: Wolgemuth & Hyatt, 1989), 198.

[4] Graham Lord, *James Herriot: The Life of a Country Vet* (New York: Carroll & Graf, 1997), 188-89.

[5] As described in James W. Moore, *Healing Where it Hurts* (Nashville: Dimensions for Living, 1993), 34-35.

[6] *Quote* 71: 102.

[7] *Quote* 68: 228.

ROADBLOCK #16

When We Put Things Off

The Procrastination Roadblock

The Procrastinators Club of America was founded in 1956 in Philadelphia when someone thought it might be funny if an organization called The Procrastinators Club was to postpone its first meeting. An announcement by the Bellevue-Stratford Hotel got the press interested, and an actual meeting became a necessity. Les Waas was the founder, and he is still the club president. The club claims a nationwide membership of more than 500,000 members. However, only about 33,000 have actually sent in their membership applications. The others are going to sometime soon. The club disciplined a member recently for sending out Christmas cards on time by kicking him out of the club. However, they later reinstated him when they discovered that the cards were actually for last Christmas. One member vowed to quit smoking. He knew it would be easy because he had never actually started smoking.

The preceding paragraph is a mixture of truth and fiction, for there really is a Procrastinators Club of America, although the other information cited above is spoof. If more of us knew about this club, however, the membership would quickly mushroom because many of us live by the motto "I'll do that tomorrow." Contrary to what one little boy said, procrastination is not just something the Presbyterians believe in (I assume he meant "predestination"?). All of us believe in procrastination at one time or another. It is in fact one of the most common personal characteristics in our lives.

Sometimes it pays off. At one church, someone procrastinated about hauling off an old piano. Then, before they could pay someone to haul it off, someone actually stole the piano and hauled it off for them—saving them some money. On such occasions as that, procrastination may pay off. However, in most cases, procrastination is a roadblock that keeps us from experiencing the abundant life Jesus wants us to experience. Time management expert Alec Mackenzie calls procrastination "a close relative of incompetence and a handmaiden of inefficiency."[1] Therefore, developing a strategy for moving around this roadblock is essential to abundant living.

Search the Scripture

For the Christian, the place to begin seeking answers is the Bible. The Bible speaks often about this specific roadblock. Here are a few verses to consider.

- Joshua 7:10: "The LORD said to Joshua, 'Stand up! What are you doing down on your face?'"
- Matthew 6:34: "Therefore do not worry about tomorrow, for tomorrow will worry about itself. Each day has enough trouble of its own."
- Romans 13:12: "The night is nearly over; the day is almost here. So let us put aside the deeds of darkness and put on the armor of light."
- 2 Corinthians 6:2: "For he says, 'In the time of my favor I heard you, and in the day of salvation I helped you.' I tell you, now is the time of God's favor, now is the day of salvation."
- 2 Corinthians 8:10-11: "And here is my advice about what is best for you in this matter: Last year you were the first not only to give but also to have the desire to do so. Now finish the work, so that your eager willingness to do it may be matched by your completion of it, according to your means."
- Philippians 3:13-14: "Brothers, I do not consider myself yet to have taken hold of it. But one thing I do: Forgetting what is behind and straining toward what is ahead, I press on toward the goal to win the prize for which God has called me heavenward in Christ Jesus."
- James 4:13-14: "Now listen, you who say, 'Today or tomorrow we will go to this or that city, spend a year there, carry on business and make money.'

Why, you do not even know what will happen tomorrow. What is your life? You are a mist that appears for a little while and then vanishes."

First of all, these Scriptures encourage us to let go of the past. Joshua had to learn that lesson early in Israel's conquest of the land of Canaan. The initial victory at Jericho was followed by a humiliating defeat at Ai. In response, Joshua fell on his face in prayer. God reminded Joshua that it was not time to mourn about what had already happened. It was instead a time to move forward (Josh 7:11). Joshua knew what the problem was and God called him to immediate action in dealing with it. "Let go of the past," God told Joshua. "It's time to move forward."

Similarly, all of us are at times paralyzed by a failure in the past. In such cases, our procrastination provides protection from further pain. At other times, we are paralyzed by a success in the past. In his short story "The Eighty-Yard Run," Irwin Shaw tells of a college freshman who, at his first football practice, broke loose for an 80-yard touchdown run. His teammates were in awe. His coach was impressed. "You're going to have a great future," the coach opined. His girlfriend rewarded him with warm kisses of congratulations. The young man was perfectly content. However, that run was the high point of his life. Nothing in the rest of his life ever lived up to that day.[2] In this case, his procrastination prevented him from future achievements.

Either as a failure that threatens repeated pain in the future or as a success that we can never top in the future, the past often robs us of the possibilities of today. Consequently, the Scriptures admonish us to let go of the past (Phil 3:13-14).

Further, these Scriptures warn us not to allow the fear of tomorrow to rob us of the joy of today. Often an anxiety about what will happen in the future paralyzes us in the present. Jesus reminded us that no one can control tomorrow. No one is even guaranteed tomorrow. All anyone has is today. And, Jesus added, each day has enough to keep us busy if we will just focus our attention on this day (Matt 6:34). Nor does anyone know when their last day will be. Therefore, the Scriptures encourage us to live out our commitment to God now (Rom 13:12; Jas 4:13-14). Review the chapter on the roadblock of anxiety for further help here. Anxiety feeds our procrastination. Therefore, combating anxiety will also help us navigate around the roadblock of procrastination.

In addition, these Scriptures urge us to press toward tomorrow. Letting go of the past is not enough, nor is simply getting started in the present. We must also persist with our action oriented toward the future. Procrastination not only prevents us from starting a task; it also prevents us from completing a task once we start it. Paul reminded the Corinthians that a good beginning is not enough without the proper follow through (2 Cor 8:10-11). Paul reflected the same thought in his memorable statement in Philippians 3:13-14. These Scriptures call us to break out of our procrastination and do something for God today, and then to continue doing something for God in each new today he gives us. We are to be persistently proactive.

Perhaps the best biblical example of this persistent proactivity is Andrew, one of the disciples of Jesus. The Gospel writers give us only a few glimpses of Andrew, but each picture shows him doing immediately what needed to be done. Let me mention three of these instances.

One day, as the wilderness preacher John was talking with two of his disciples, Jesus came by. John identified Jesus as the special person from God about whom he had been telling his disciples. The Bible says, "When the two disciples heard him say this, they followed Jesus" (John 1:37). One of those two was Andrew. Andrew had heard what John had said and was anticipating the coming of this special man from God. When this special man came, Andrew did not say, "I am going to follow him someday." Rather, Andrew followed him immediately.

Then, after an extended conversation with Jesus, Andrew became convinced that Jesus was the Messiah. The Bible says, "The first thing Andrew did was to find his brother Simon and tell him, 'We have found the Messiah' (that is, the Christ). And he brought him to Jesus" (John 1:41-42). Andrew recognized Jesus as the special agent sent from God who could make an eternal difference in a person's life. When he recognized who Jesus was, Andrew did not say, "I am going to tell my brother about him someday." Instead, Andrew told his brother immediately.

The third verse that reflects on Andrew's spirit of persistent proactivity is John 6:9. Remember the context. When Jesus taught on the mountain, thousands of people gathered to listen. Hours passed. Eventually, when the people became hungry, Jesus instructed the disciples to feed them. Philip debated with Jesus how it was possible to accomplish that monumental task of feeding this multitude of people, since it would take so much money to buy the needed supplies, and they had no resources available. Not Andrew. Andrew looked around, found a boy with a lunch, and brought the boy to Jesus. He did not say, "After a while I am going to see what I can do to help the situation." Instead, Andrew did something immediately.

Andrew might not have had the "star quality" of his brother Peter. However, Andrew demonstrated a commitment to immediate action that prevented procrastination from ever taking root in his life. Andrew clearly models what it takes to move around the roadblock of procrastination.

Set the Strategy

So from these specific Scriptures and from the example of Andrew, we can hammer out strategies that will enable us to move from procrastination to proactivity. Let me identify four strategies.

Strategy #1 is to *map out a plan*. Procrastination is a choice. It is a deliberate choice to do nothing. Consequently, the antidote to procrastination is the choice to do something. Mapping out a plan means deciding what we want to do and how we will accomplish it.

Every one of us who has eaten a Wendy's hamburger is glad that David Thomas developed his popular fast food restaurant. What we sometimes forget is that Dave made the decision that he wanted to be a successful restaurant owner at the age of eight![3] Today, more than four thousand Wendy's restaurants are located all over the world, but it started with an eight-year-old boy who dreamed that he would one day own the best restaurant in the world. The next time procrastination begins to take control of your life, sit with pen and paper and write down specific things you need to do. Map out a plan.

Strategy #2 is to *set a deadline*. Procrastination likes to live on "Someday Isle." "Someday I'll do this" or "Someday I'll do that." Consequently, one antidote for procrastination is to set specific deadlines for when things have to be done. Entertainment entrepreneur Nolan Bushnell affirms that part of what has made American business successful is the "trade show phenomenon." He explains, "The fact that twice a year the creative talent of this country is working until midnight to get something ready for a trade show is very good for the economy."[4]

The "trade show phenomenon" happens for me as a pastor every week as Sunday approaches. Nothing presses a pastor into action quite as quickly as the fact that Sunday is coming and expectant people will gather at the place of worship to hear what he has to say. The recognition of what I call the IROS factor—the incessant return of the Sabbath—spurs me out of my procrastination early in the week to begin to put my sermon together.

This must be a part of the strategy for moving around the roadblock of procrastination. As you map out your plans, set deadlines. Determine certain times when certain things have to be done. These deadlines will serve as procrastination-busters.

Strategy #3 is to *develop some accountability*. Procrastination says, "No one cares what I do, so I'll just do nothing." Consequently, another antidote for procrastination is to make ourselves accountable to another person or to a group of people. These accountability partners must understand our personal vision. They must recognize what it will look like when this personal vision is fulfilled. And they must care enough about us to keep us accountable.

An old adage suggests, "People do what you inspect, not what you expect." That is true of all of us. The responsibility to give a report to someone about our lives will help move us out of our procrastination into proactivity.

Strategy #4 is to *take the first step*. Procrastination says, "It's too hard to go the whole distance." Consequently, an antidote for procrastination is to recognize that the whole distance begins with the first step, and the journey of life must be taken one step at a time. After the first step has been taken, the rest will follow.

Fitzgerald Kennedy, grandfather of former President John F. Kennedy, grew up in Ireland. He came home from school each day with a whole group of boys. They walked along a jagged, high cobblestone fence. The boys talked about climbing over that fence but never did. One day, as they were walking home from school, Fitzgerald took off his cap and threw it over the wall. Then he climbed over the fence to get it. The moment he threw his hat over the wall, he knew he had to climb over to get it back, because he didn't dare go home without his cap.[4]

Sometimes a similar strategy will snap us out of the daze of our procrastination. Sometimes the challenges of life overwhelm us. Paralysis sets in. At such moments, throwing our hat over the fence—that is, taking a first step—will get us started in fulfilling the challenges before us.

Final Word

In a recent cartoon, Garfield said, "One of my pet peeves is someone who doesn't finish what he starts." In the next frame, he adds, "I'm not one of those people." In the final frame, he explains, "I just never start anything." Garfield would be a good member of the Procrastinators Club. In contrast, those who move around the roadblock of procrastination are those who will implement strategies similar to the ones listed above. All we have is today. Let's make the most of it.

Prayer

O Timeless God
We know that you are the God
Of past, present, and future.

Help us to live
In the present,
Out of the past and
Into the future.

Most of all,
Help us to claim today
And live it to the fullest.

Amen.

NOTES

[1] R. Alec Mackenzie, *The Time Trap* (New York: McGraw-Hill Book Company, 1972), 35.

[2] As quoted in Harold Kushner, *When All You've Ever Wanted Isn't Enough* (New York: Pocket Books, 1986), 71.

[3] R. David Thomas, *Dave's Way* (New York: Berkley Books, 1991), 3.

[4] As noted in John C. Maxwell, *Be All You Can Be!* (Wheaton IL: Victor Books, 1987), 42.

When We Feel Sorry for Ourselves

The Self-Pity Roadblock

A rising young executive was on his way to work in New York City. He lived in the suburbs and had to take the subway into the city each day. He stood on the ramp where the train would pass with his $1,500 suit, his $300 shoes, a pipe in his mouth, and a leather attaché case in his hand. This man was on the rise. He had the world by the tail. Watch out, world! On the subway was another man who was on his way into the city, except that he was not on top of his world. In fact, he was nauseated and felt terrible. He was the first one on the subway, but at each stop, more people got on. The heat of the bodies and the claustrophobia heightened by the increased number in the car were about to get the best of this man. Finally, he lost it. With a hand over his mouth, he used his other hand to fight his way to the door of the car. Just as he reached the door, the train stopped at the station where the rising young business executive was standing. When the door opened, the sick traveler threw up all over the rising young executive, all over his $1,500 suit, all over his expensive shoes, on his pipe, and on his attaché case. Before either of the men could move, the doors of the subway slammed shut, and the train moved away from the area. As the sick man looked out the window at the rising young executive standing there, he could read his lips as he said, "Why me?"

A lot of people are saying that in our world today. Instead of facing challenges and moving through them, many today have settled into a continuous pity party. "Why me?" is the most popular chorus of our day. And it is a roadblock that is preventing many Christians from experiencing the full and abundant life God wants us to experience. Learning how to move around this roadblock is essential to abundant living.

Search the Scripture

For the Christian, the place to begin in seeking answers is the Bible. Multiple Scriptures will help us when self-pity lurks in our lives. Let me list some of them.

- Psalm 73:16-17: "When I pondered to understand this, it was troublesome in my sight until I came into the sanctuary of God."
- Psalm 118:24: "This is the day the LORD has made; let us rejoice and be glad in it."
- Isaiah 41:10: "So do not fear, for I am with you; do not be dismayed, for I am your God. I will strengthen you and help you; I will uphold you with my righteous right hand."
- Isaiah 59:1: "Behold, the LORD's hand is not so short that it cannot save; neither is his ear so dull that it cannot hear."
- Matthew 6:34: "Therefore do not worry about tomorrow, for tomorrow will worry about itself. Each day has enough trouble of its own."
- Romans 8:18: "For I consider that the sufferings of this present time are not worthy to be compared with the glory that is to be revealed to us."
- Romans 8:28: "And we know that God causes all things to work together for good to those who love God, to those who are called according to his purpose."
- Romans 14:12: "So then, each of us will give an account of himself to God."
- 2 Corinthians 12:10: "Therefore I am well content with weaknesses, with insults, with distresses, with persecutions, with difficulties, for Christ's sake; for when I am weak, then I am strong."

- Philippians 2:4: "Each of you should look not only to your own interests, but also to the interests of others."
- Philippians 4:19: "And my God will meet all your needs according to his glorious riches in Christ Jesus."

First of all, these Scriptures underscore the importance of perspective. On the one hand, every person must live in the present tense. It is unproductive to spend our time either longing for a yesterday that is past or yearning for a future that is not yet here. That is why the psalmist reminded us to "rejoice" in today (Ps 118:24) and why Jesus challenged us to live in today (Matt 6:34). Today is all we have for sure. That should be the starting point for all of us. And yet, as Christians, our lives have a larger context than just today (Rom 8:28). Consequently, Christians need to evaluate present realities in light of our future accountability to God, as I asserted in the last chapter (Rom 14:12). Likewise, Christians need to recognize our connectedness to those who have gone before us (Heb 13:7). Viewing life from this larger perspective will enable us to evaluate our current circumstances more realistically.

In addition, these Scriptures highlight the importance of focus. Self-pity often grows out of a wrong focus. At times, all of us focus too much on ourselves. The Bible urges us instead to focus on others (Phil 2:4). Contrast the generous spirit of Barnabas, who focused on how he could help others (Acts 4:36-37), with the conniving spirits of Ananias and Sapphira, who focused on how they could get glory for themselves (Acts 5:1-11). What a difference focus makes!

All of us also focus too much on our own meager resources. The Bible urges us instead to remember God's abundant resources (Phil 4:19). Redirecting our focus on God's abundance can often shake us out of our pity party. In Psalm 73, the psalmist whines about the inequities of life. However, coming into the presence of a gracious God puts his problem into proper perspective (Ps 73:16-17). Again, the Scripture acknowledges the difference focus makes.

Further, these Scriptures remind us of the importance of trust. The prophet Isaiah repeatedly reminded his contemporaries of the importance of trusting God (Isa 41; Isa 10; 59:1). Mother Teresa repeatedly illustrated in her life what it meant to trust God. Then she articulated what it meant to trust God in her oft-repeated statement: "You will never know that Jesus is all you need until Jesus is all you've got."[1] Trust in God is also the beginning point of wisdom, as the writer of Proverbs affirmed (3:4-5). And trusting God is a key factor in moving around the roadblock of self-pity.

One of the most intriguing biblical examples of someone who avoided self-pity was Joseph. If ever a person had the right to feel sorry for himself, Joseph did. He was apparently somewhat obnoxious in the way he acted toward his brothers early on. He received the special favor of his father and held that over his brothers' heads. He evidently did not have to work like his brothers did. In addition, Joseph had special dreams in which he envisioned his brothers bowing down to him. He was obnoxious toward them to be sure. Yet, Joseph did not deserve the treatment meted out by his brothers. His brothers dug a pit and threw him into it, planning to leave him there to die. Joseph was saved from this fate only to be pushed into a worse fate. He was sold as a slave. The pampered, spoiled rich boy who could do anything he wanted now had to do what he was told. Everyone who has heard this story would agree the things that happened to Joseph were not fair. Consequently, Joseph could have settled into a lifelong pity party, but he didn't.

Instead, he exerted himself as a slave, caught the attention of his master, and eventually rose to an important position in Potiphar's house. At that point, Potiphar's wife tried to seduce Joseph. Joseph refused her overtures because he knew that giving in would be wrong toward God and wrong toward his master. As a result, Potiphar's wife accused Joseph of trying to rape her, and Joseph was thrown into an Egyptian dungeon. Moral, committed Joseph who refused to do what was wrong was punished for his commitment. Again, everyone would agree the things that happened to Joseph were not fair. And again, Joseph could have settled into a lifelong pity party, but he didn't.

Instead, Joseph continued to watch for opportunities for advancement, even in jail. He interpreted the dreams of one of his fellow inmates correctly, and that inmate promised to help him out of jail. But then for two years Joseph did not hear from this man. For two years Joseph continued to languish in the Egyptian prison. Joseph did a favor for this man, but this man refused to return the favor. Again, the treatment Joseph received was not fair. And again, Joseph could have settled into a lifelong pity party, but he didn't.

That was the pattern of Joseph's life. One unexpected setback after another shattered his hopes and dreams. Yet, Joseph refused to give in to self-pity. Instead—because of his perspective, his focus, and his trust—he continued to live out his life of faith. He is a model of the principles identified in the Scriptures cited above. He is also an inspiration for us as we put together a strategy for moving around this roadblock of self-pity today.

Set the Strategy

Let me outline specific strategies for moving around this roadblock so that we can experience the fullness of life God has made available to us through Jesus.

Strategy #1 is to *look at ourselves with a wide-angle lens.* I have a zoom lens on my camera. When I zoom in on a particular object, it seems bigger than it really is because the zoom takes the object out of its true context and magnifies it. However, when I pull the zoom lens in and simply look through the viewer, the object does not seem as large as it was and it is no longer seen in isolation from its context. If, on the other hand, I look at the object through a wide-angle lens, I get the opposite effect. The object seems smaller and less significant than it is because it is placed in the context of a larger picture.

These simple truths from the field of photography illustrate our first strategy in dealing with self-pity. The key is to look at life through a wide-angle lens, not through a zoom lens. Looking through the zoom lens will magnify our problems and make them appear to be larger than life. On the other hand, looking at our situation through a wide-angle lens will reduce the apparent size of our problem by setting it in a larger context. Setting the problem in a larger context reminds us that our problem does not compare to the blessings already experienced in the past, nor does it compare to the promises to be fulfilled in the future.

This is the first strategy for moving around the roadblock of self-pity. When life seems to be unfair, remember the special blessings of the past and remember the yet unrealized special blessings of the future. This is what it means to look at our lives with a wide-angle lens.

Strategy #2 is to *look at God through 3-D glasses.* Some of the most entertaining times of my childhood were spent watching 3-D movies at the theatre on Saturday morning, when the special glasses literally made objects seem to jump out from the screen. These special glasses enabled us to see multiple dimensions of action instead of simply seeing the actions in one dimension. To put it another way, the special glasses enabled us to observe depths of action that ordinarily could not be discerned. IMAX and High Definition Television provide similar dynamics today.

This childhood experience needs to be duplicated in our lives today in order for us to move around the roadblock of self-pity. Our tendency is to look at life with one-dimensional vision, seeing only the discouraging realities playing out right in front of us. However, using our three-dimensional glasses will enable us to observe depths of reality that escaped our first glance.

Let me illustrate how this works in our lives. Suppose that a ten-year-old boy goes into a bicycle shop with his dad. As they browse, a certain bike catches the boy's eye. He tells his dad this is a bike he would like to have, but his dad refuses to get it for him. For weeks, the little boy throws a pity party, moping around the house feeling sorry for himself. But then, on Christmas day, he discovers a bicycle sitting next to the Christmas tree with a ribbon wrapped around the handlebars and his name on it; it is a much more expensive bicycle with more bells and whistles than the one he had desired. At that point, this boy finally discerns the reason his father had not given him the other bike when he asked for it. His father had something better in mind to give him. The boy did not recognize all his father was planning to do. He needed to put on his 3-D glasses!

That often happens to us. All we can see is the flat picture of our immediate situation. The key is to get a better view of what is happening in our lives by putting on our 3-D glasses. Whenever life seems to be unfair, looking at our situation through 3-D glasses will enable us to recognize the plans our heavenly Father has for us, plans bigger than our desires that God will give us in his timing, which is also better than ours. We need to look at God through 3-D glasses.

Strategy #3 is to *look at others with x-ray vision*. In 1895, when W. C. Roentgen, professor at Wurzburg, discovered a ray whose nature he could not distinctly identify, he borrowed from algebra the letter used to designate an unknown item, calling it the x-ray.[2] The x-ray was an amazing discovery, one that enables us to see things we had never seen before with the human eye. With the x-ray, we can see past the external surface and can actually see what is inside a person.

X-ray vision is also a valuable tool in moving past the roadblock of self-pity. Our self-pity is often fed by a comparison between us and others. Based on the surface view, the lives of others usually seem better and more rewarding and more enjoyable than ours. However, penetrating the surface and discovering what is going on at a deeper level in their lives through x-ray vision will reveal that they have hurts just like us, needs just like ours, and problems just like the ones in our lives. So when our self-pity is stimulated by the apparent blessings of others, the key is to remember that others have problems just like we do. We need to look at others with x-ray vision.

Final Word

We often say, "What we focus on determines what we see." That is true. But the other day, I heard a different version of that statement. Someone said, "What we focus on determines what we miss."[3] That, too, is true. Focusing on the right things—in our lives, in God, and in the lives of others—will help us miss the things that cause us to envelop our lives in self-pity and help us see the things that will enable us to have productive lives of service.

Prayer

Dear Loving Father
Who has given us so much
We give you thanks.

Thank you for loving us
Even when we are unlovely
And for providing for us
Even when we are ungrateful
And for forgiving us
Even when we are undeserving.

Instead of always desiring more
Help us to use more effectively
What we already have.

Amen.

NOTES

[1] As retold in Anthony Campolo, *Seven Deadly Sins* (Wheaton: Victor, 1987), 130.

[2] Joseph T. Shipley, *Dictionary of Word Origins* (New York: Dorset Press, 1945), 395.

[3] Eric Allenbaugh, *Wake-up Calls* (Austin: Discovery Publications, 1992), 35.

Quick Review

ROADBLOCK #1

When We Want Too Much Too Soon
The Ambition Roadblock

Search the Scripture
   Psalm 119:36-37
   Luke 12:15
   Romans 12:3
   Philippians 4:11
   1 Timothy 6:10
   Hebrews 13:5-6

Our Lessons
   The reasons for our drivenness
   The irony of our drivenness
   The nature of our drivenness

Our Model
   Absalom

Set the Strategy
   Strategy #1: Determine where our drivenness comes from.
   Strategy #2: Develop the proper response to the cause of our drivenness.
   Strategy #3: Acknowledge and accept the limitations of life.

For more information, see page 1.

ROADBLOCK #2

When We're Good and Mad
The Anger Roadblock

Search the Scripture
> Job 5:2
> Proverbs 14:17a
> Proverbs 16:32
> Proverbs 19:19
> Proverbs 25:28
> Ecclesiastes 7:9
> Ephesians 4:26
> James 1:20

Our Lessons
> Anger can be destructive.
> Anger can be addictive.
> Anger can be controlled.

Our Model
> Joseph

Set the Strategy
> Strategy #1: Delay the expression of our anger.
> Strategy #2: Define the reason for our anger.
> Strategy #3: Destroy the root of our anger.

For more information, see page 9.

ROADBLOCK #3

When We're Tied Up in Knots
The Anxiety Roadblock

Search the Scripture
    Matthew 6:25
    Matthew 6:34
    Matthew 13:22
    John 14:1
    Philippians 4:6-7
    1 Peter 5:6-7

Our Lessons
    The sources of anxiety
    The danger of anxiety
    The solutions for anxiety

Our Model
    Mary

Set the Strategy
    Strategy #1: Refocus on God.
    Strategy #2: Put our anxiety in perspective.
    Strategy #3: Simplify our lives.
    Strategy #4: Get busy doing something.

For more information, see page 17.

ROADBLOCK #4

When We're in a Rut
The Boredom Roadblock

Search the Scripture
 Genesis 12:1
 Psalm 34:8
 Proverbs 1:5; 16:22
 Matthew 10:16; 18:13
 Luke 5:38
 Luke 16:8
 1 Peter 1:13

Our Lessons
 The necessity of faith
 The necessity of wisdom
 The necessity of change

Our Model
 Ruth

Set the Strategy
 Strategy #1: Challenge the rules.
 Strategy #2: Reverse the process.
 Strategy #3: Move beyond our borders.
 Strategy #4: Lighten up.

For more information, see page 25.

ROADBLOCK #5

When We Don't Have Time
The Busyness Roadblock

Search the Scripture
    Psalms 25:5; 27:14
    Psalms 37:7; 90:12
    Ecclesiastes 2:4-6,11
    Isaiah 5:11-12
    Isaiah 40:31
    Mark 6:31

Our Lessons
    The danger of our busyness
    The reasons for our busyness
    The result of our busyness
    The antidote for our busyness

Our Model
    Jethro

Set the Strategy
    Strategy #1: Evaluate
    Strategy #2: Eliminate
    Strategy #3: Delegate
    Strategy #4: Orchestrate

For more information, see page 33.

ROADBLOCK #6

When We Can't Say What We Mean
The Communication Roadblock

Search the Scripture
   Psalms 19:14; 141:3
   Proverbs 4:1; 15:23; 25:11
   Ecclesiastes 10:12
   Matthew 5:37; 12:36
   Ephesians 4:29
   James 3:7-8

Our Lessons
   The accountability for our communication
   The difficulty of communication
   The importance of our communication

Our Model
   Nehemiah

Set the Strategy
   Strategy #1: Learn how to listen empathetically.
   Strategy #2: Develop our relationships.
   Strategy #3: Participate in face-to-face dialogues.
   Strategy #4: Be sensitive to nonverbal clues.

For more information, see page 41.

ROADBLOCK #7

When Others Don't Like What We Do
The Criticism Roadblock

Search the Scripture
    Psalm 102:8
    Proverbs 11:11; 23:12; 28:13
    Matthew 7:1
    Romans 14:10; 14:13
    Ephesians 4:2
    James 4:11

Our Lessons
    Criticism is universal.
    Criticism can be helpful.
    Criticism can be harmful.
    Criticism is contagious.

Our Model
    Jeremiah

Set the Strategy
    Strategy #1: Realization
    Strategy #2: Evaluation
    Strategy #3: Contemplation
    Strategy #4: Activation

For more information, see page 49.

ROADBLOCK #8

When We Feel Boxed In
The Depression Roadblock

Search the Scripture
> Psalms 30:5; 31:24
> Isaiah 43:2-3
> Matthew 11:28; Luke 18:1
> Romans 8:18
> 2 Corinthians 1:3; 4:8-10
> Philippians 4:13

Our Lessons
> There is more to life than just today.
> There is more to life than just our own resources.
> There is more to life than just our own problems.

Our Model
> Job

Set the Strategy
> Strategy #1: Check our physical condition.
> Strategy #2: Confess our sin.
> Strategy #3: Clarify our standards.
> Strategy #4: Build strong relationships.
> Strategy #5: Seek help from a professional counselor.

For more information, see page 57.

ROADBLOCK #9

When Others Get What We Want
The Envy Roadblock

Search the Scripture
    Job 5:2
    Psalm 118:24
    Proverbs 14:30; 27:4
    Ecclesiastes 4:4
    1 Corinthians 13:4
    Philippians 4:11
    James 3:16
    1 Peter 2:1

Our Lessons
    Life is a gift.
    Envy is destructive.
    Love and envy are incompatible.

Our Model
    John the Baptizer

Set the Strategy
    Strategy #1: Contemplate the goodness of God.
    Strategy #2: Establish separate accounts.
    Strategy #3: Avoid comparisons.

For more information, see page 65.

ROADBLOCK #10

When We Blow It
The Failure Roadblock

Search the Scripture
    Psalm 37:24
    Jonah 3:1
    John 8:10-11
    Romans 8:38-39
    Galatians 6:1
    1 John 1:9

Our Lessons
    God is a God of the second chance.
    Our failures are limited.
    We must be willing to give others a second chance.

Our Model
    John Mark

Set the Strategy
    Strategy #1: Think the right thoughts.
    Strategy #2: Ask the right questions.
    Strategy #3: Do the right things.

For more information, see page 73.

ROADBLOCK #11

When We Feel Too Bad to Feel Good
The Guilt Roadblock

Search the Scripture
> Psalms 38:4; 103:12
> Isaiah 1:18; 6:5
> Jeremiah 33:8
> Malachi 3:7
> Matthew 4:17; Luke 5:8
> 1 John 1:9

Our Lessons
> The reality of guilt
> The remedy for guilt
> The results of that remedy for guilt

Our Model
> David

Set the Strategy
> Strategy #1: Avoid inappropriate strategies.
> Strategy #2: Clarify the source and nature of our guilt.
> Strategy #3: Confess to God.
> Strategy #4: Change our actions.

For more information, see page 81.

ROADBLOCK #12

When We Can't Get Out of Bed
The Immobilization Roadblock

Search the Scripture
    Ecclesiastes 9:10; 11:6
    Jeremiah 31:29-30
    Luke 12:48
    1 Corinthians 3:12-15
    James 4:13
    2 Peter 3:11-12

Our Lessons
    Time is short.
    Results are uncertain.
    Everyone is responsible.
    Judgment is certain.

Our Model
    Paul

Set the Strategy
    Strategy #1: Cultivate our inner life.
    Strategy #2: Strengthen our connections.
    Strategy #3: Clarify our goals.
    Strategy #4: Sharpen our focus.

For more information, see page 89.

ROADBLOCK #13

When We Have to Choose
The Indecisiveness Roadblock

Search the Scripture
Psalm 119:97-100
Proverbs 3:5-6; 13:20; 15:22
John 16:13
Philippians 4:6-7

Our Lessons
The importance of God's word
The importance of faith
The importance of our peers
The importance of the Holy Spirit
The importance of prayer

Our Model
Gideon

Set the Strategy
Strategy #1: Refine our focus.
Strategy #2: Clarify our options.
Strategy #3: Establish some guidelines.
Strategy #4: Consider the consequences.
Strategy #5: Seek counsel.
Strategy #6: Be willing to adjust.

For more information, see page 97.

ROADBLOCK #14

When We Feel All Alone
The Loneliness Roadblock

Search the Scripture
    Genesis 2:18
    Deuteronomy 31:8
    Joshua 1:9
    Psalms 16:8b; 23:4; 46:10; 139:7-10
    Isaiah 43:2
    Matthew 28:20b
    Mark 8:35
    Hebrews 12:1-2

Our Lessons
    The impossibility of aloneness
    The value of loneliness
    The danger of loneliness

Our Model
    Elijah

Set the Strategy
    Strategy #1: Practice the presence of God.
    Strategy #2: Develop a proper understanding of loneliness.
    Strategy #3: Do something for others.
    Strategy #4: Remember our connectedness.

For more information, see page 105.

ROADBLOCK #15

When We Think Too Highly of Ourselves
The Pride Roadblock

Search the Scripture
   Deuteronomy 8:18
   Psalm 101:5b
   Proverbs 16:5; 16:18
   Ecclesiastes 4:9-12
   Romans 12:3
   1 Corinthians 4:7; 10:12
   Galatians 6:3
   Philippians 2:3
   James 1:17; 4:6

Our Lessons
   The dominance of pride
   The deception of pride
   The danger of pride

Our Model
   Daniel

Set the Strategy
   Strategy #1: Distinguish between positive pride and negative pride.
   Strategy #2: Remember where we came from.
   Strategy #3: Remember where we are going.

For more information, see page 113.

ROADBLOCK #16

When We Put Things Off
The Procrastination Roadblock

Search the Scripture
Joshua 7:10
Matthew 6:34
Romans 13:12
2 Corinthians 6:2
2 Corinthians 8:10-11
Philippians 3:13-14
James 4:13-14

Our Lessons
Let go of the past.
Do not fear the future.
Press toward tomorrow.

Our Model
Andrew

Set the Strategy
Strategy #1: Map out a plan.
Strategy #2: Set a deadline.
Strategy #3: Develop some accountability.
Strategy #4: Take the first step.

For more information, see page 121.

ROADBLOCK #17

When We Feel Sorry for Ourselves
The Self-Pity Roadblock

Search the Scripture
    Psalms 73:16-17; 118:24
    Isaiah 41:10; 59:1
    Matthew 6:34
    Romans 8:18; 8:28; 14:12
    2 Corinthians 12:10
    Philippians 2:4; 4:19

Our Lessons
    The importance of perspective
    The importance of focus
    The importance of trust

Our Model
    Joseph

Set the Strategy
    Strategy #1: Look at ourselves with a wide-angle lens.
    Strategy #2: Look at God through 3-D glasses.
    Strategy #3: Look at others with x-ray vision.

For more information, see page 129.

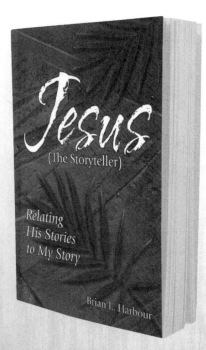
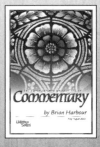